French Bliss

Joni Sutton and Chip Williams

Published by Chip Williams, 2021.

FRENCH BLISS

First edition. June 1, 2021.

ISBN: 979-8201100599

Written by Joni Sutton and Chip Williams.

Table of Contents

Have you ever dreamt of living in a foreign country?

Follow two intrepid Minnesota retirees as they learn what it takes to live like a local in France. Read about their adventures in their adopted country- the humorous encounters, the obstacles they overcame, and the life-long friends they made along the way. Whether your interest is France, travel, wine, local history or just an entertaining story, you will find this book an appealing read.

Praise for "French Bliss"

"If you've ever dreamed of living in France, this is your chance to live vicariously through the eyes of this charming American couple, Chip and Joni, and to share in their real life observations of this experience. Then, get your passports ready!"

Ginny Blackwell, President/CEO, Intl. Property Shares

"Stow away with Joni and Chip as they embark on an unforgettable adventure. Rather than having a "tourist" experience, they immerse themselves in village life. As foreign residents in a new land, there are bound to be a few mishaps, frustrations, and of course incredible discoveries. They candidly share them all, with wit and wisdom. The highs and lows tug at your heart strings, as Joni, Chip and their new French "family" feel like old friends."

Traci Parent, Creator of frenchdetours.com

Acknowledgement

We would be terribly remiss if we did not acknowledge the contributions to this book by our French friends. They are like family to us. Without their kindness, patience, knowledge, humor, and caring attitude, we most likely would not have lasted one week in their country. Words are not enough to relay our gratitude to them. We dedicate this book to them.

To protect their privacy, we have changed names and, in some cases, locations.

Il ne faudrait surtout pas omettre les contributions de nos amis français à ce livre. Ils sont comme une famille pour nous. Sans leur gentillesse, leur patience, leurs connaissances, leur sens d'humour et leur bienveillance, nous n'aurions sans doute pas survécu une semaine dans leur pays. Les mots ne suffisant pas à transmettre notre gratitude, nous leur dédions donc ce livre.

Pour protéger leur vie privée, nous avons changé les noms et, dans certains cas, les lieux.

Prélude (Joni)

When I was five or six years old, there was an evening when my parents went out. This was a rare event for them, and my older sister and her friend were my babysitters. When it was time for bed, I didn't want to go to sleep and I wanted my mom to be the one to tuck me in. My sister and her friend hadn't paid attention to me all night, and now that I'm thinking about it, maybe the reason I couldn't go to sleep was because they might have put me to bed an hour or two earlier than they should have. At any rate, my sister came into the bedroom when she heard me crying, and she talked me down. She told me to just shut my eyes and think about something good, and I'd be able to go to sleep.

"But I can't think of anything good," I said.

"Imagine that you are in France. Imagine that you are seeing the Eiffel Tower."

And so it began. I went to sleep that night dreaming of being in France. I have done that hundreds, if not thousands, of times since that night. My sister planted a small idea in my childhood brain, and that idea took hold. I bought "Learn to Speak French" paperbacks at the bookstore and slowly learned to say a variety of French phrases, pronounced in a way that no French person would ever be able to comprehend. I forced my dad to be my student while I pretended to be the French teacher. Before long he, too, was successfully mispronouncing many French phrases. I wanted to become a flight attendant (actually, in those days it would have been a stewardess). I saw this as a glamorous job for young women who were beautiful and sophisticated, who wanted to see the world and who would no doubt meet the dignified and wealthy man of their dreams while in the air. My wealthy dreamboat would have a home in France.

When I was in high school, I did not, however, get started with French classes. In ninth grade there was the option to take German after school for students who wanted to be able to take more classes than the ordinary school day would allow. In spite of not really being interested in learning German, I was very interested in learning a language. I joined twenty-five students after school every day for an entire school year and began memorizing my German dialogues. Soon I was able to talk about Reinhardt going skiing and about having bratwurst with potatoes for lunch. It may interest you to know that in German there are nine different forms of the word "the," depending not only on the gender of the noun, but also upon where the noun is in the sentence. No? It didn't interest me either, so after two years of being frustrated with "the," I switched to French.

I now learned to pronounce those French phrases from my childhood a little less poorly. Better still, the French teachers at school decided to take a group of their students to France in the summer. These days this is a common occurrence, but back in 1970 it was a nearly revolutionary idea. We were going for five weeks.

The cost for the trip, including airfare from New York, was $600. I couldn't believe that my parents were actually going to be shelling out that kind of money for me to go to France. My classmates and I did what we could to help defray the cost by collecting soda bottles and newspapers, and by holding garage sales.

The big day arrived, and off we went to Strasbourg, France, taking classes in the morning and exploring the city in the afternoon. We ate cow's tongue, flaming bananas and chocolate mousse. In Paris we climbed the stairs to the second level of the Eiffel Tower. We bought liqueur-filled chocolates at the candy store (by accident) and hated them. For me, the five weeks went by quickly. On the day before we went home, I realized that all of my friends couldn't wait to get back to the States, and this came as a total shock to me. I clearly remember going off on my own for a long walk around the neighborhoods of Strasbourg (this was a different time, when students could go off on their own and no one even needed to be told about it), wondering about two things: Why does everyone else want to go home, and how am I going to get back here?

Well, I did go home, but I also managed to get back to France. As a matter of fact, in college I was able to go back three times thanks to multiple summer jobs and cheap hostels. I went again after my first year of teaching. Every time it was tough for me to come home. When I travelled to Europe with my college concert band, our director made sure to check the cabin of the plane before we left Paris for home. "Where's Joni? Did she get on?" My love of all things French was common knowledge. A few years later I was fortunate enough to become involved with an organization that takes talented high school musicians to Europe for a concert tour, and I began going to Europe with them every two years. It still wasn't enough.

My dream was to *live* in France. Not to be a tourist in France, not to be a student in a dormitory in France, but to live among the French. I imagine everyone reading this has a dream of some sort: an unrealistic, out of this world, an "I'm-too-old-and-not rich-enough" type of dream. Luckily for me, I have a husband with the last name of Williams who thought himself quite clever. He told me a long time ago, "Where there's a Williams there's a way." In the years I've known him, I've learned to step aside once he has a goal in mind because nothing is going to get in the way of him achieving his goal. Once I had articulated my dream to him, and he had visited Europe and France several times himself, it became his dream as well.

Although we could not afford to move permanently to France, we decided that two or three months at a time would allow us to get to know how it felt to live there. Money was saved and research was done. I started taking French classes at the Alliance Française to improve upon my French and that bad pronunciation I taught myself when I was a child. All that remained was to wait anxiously for the time when we could both retire from our jobs and put the plan into action. That time finally came in the spring of 2011, when I retired from my teaching job, a year after my husband had done the same. In September of that same year, we packed our (many) bags, grabbed our passports, and with both excitement and fear, hopped on the plane.

What you are about to read is the story of how we planned for and spent our time in France over the course of, not only our three-month stay in 2011, but also of other subsequent falls in France. Yes, we have managed to return for extended trips several times. Some of our chapters are narrative, some are reflective, and some, we hope, will give you a laugh or two. The book is written in three parts: "Reconnaissance" tells about our preparations for a three month stay; "Bon Voyage" is about our first fall; "Encore" is about voyages to France that followed that first wonderful fall.

Our hope is that we can inspire others to follow their wildest dreams. If you don't have any, perhaps you should talk to your spouse, your partner, your best friend or your big sister to get started on one.

Part One- Reconnaissance

1- Finding our French "Home" (Chip)

As Joni wrote, we had discussed an extended trip to live in Europe on many occasions. It was now time to make these discussions become reality. In stepped "Mr. Type A" (as Joni calls me) to create a plan.

I'm going to apologize right now to those of you who are looking for reading that is more entertaining. As a step-by-step person, *I* find this all quite riveting. If you don't, just skip to chapter 3.

We began by roughing out a timeline. Although this went through several permutations, we pretty much had in mind from the beginning that we would go in the fall of the year. This would be determined by our ultimate retirements from teaching. Both Joni and I were band directors/music teachers. As we approached the retirement age in Minnesota, a target year came into focus.

"Why wait until fall?" you ask. As I had done the year before, Joni really wanted to be home in Minnesota for the beginning of the school year after her retirement. This is a truly glorious time for newly retired teachers! She wanted to experience Labor Day weekend without a big knot in her stomach about the start of school. She also wanted to participate in some of the rituals retired teachers do on the first day of classes in the fall. A group of her retired friends would gather at a restaurant for breakfast and wave at the school buses as they went by. Another cadre had a special luncheon on that day that lasted several hours instead of 27 minutes as at school. Some of my retired teacher-friends hold a Champagne breakfast on the first day of school each fall.

To that end, we determined that we would depart for France sometime around the middle of September. Since the goal here was to immerse ourselves into life in France we wanted a good chunk of time, but how long? Originally, we thought two months would be enough. We would then be home in time for Thanksgiving. Several things, however, came up that caused us to lengthen our trip.

We had started our plans with two side-trips in mind. The first of these was to attend Oktoberfest with some friends from Düsseldorf. About five years earlier, while drinking beer along the Rhine River, we had made a pact with them- the first fall we were all retired we would meet in Munich for that experience. (More on that in another chapter.)

The other trip we wanted to make was to the Beaujolais area of France for the release party of *Beaujolais Nouveau*. This event is held yearly on the third Thursday in November. This was going to add a week to our trip. Out came the pencil and we filled in another week on the calendar with big "F-R-A-N-C-E" letters.

The next extension of our planned trip occurred after we had picked a location in which to stay. I am jumping ahead in our tale a bit but it is necessary. Very near the location we finally settle on, there is a well-known wine festival that occurs late in November. Once we discovered the dates for this festival on the internet, we realized it was the weekend immediately after our scheduled departure. The pencil came out again on another week- "F-R-A-N-C-E".

At this point we realized we were not going to be home for Thanksgiving. Debating and deciding in our own minds that our families could survive without us for one Turkey Day, we decided to again add some time to our adventure. This time it was to take in several of the Christmas Markets that began around the end of November. More marks on the calendar, but we agreed that three months was the limit. Besides, that is the length of time the French legally allowed visitors without a long-term visa.

Interwoven into our discussion on the length of our stay in Europe was another big decision- *Where to live?*- in the country, a big city, small village, house, apartment?

It should be noted here that we also could have chosen to stay in another country. The western part of Switzerland is French speaking, as is Belgium. As she wrote in the previous chapter, Joni's longtime love affair with France made it her first choice. I was more torn in my thinking. I loved the mountains and sheer beauty of Switzerland. A large chunk of my family emigrated from there to the USA in the mid 1800s (that is a story for another time). One of my other loves is wine. I dabble in amateur winemaking myself. I have done lots of reading and research (read "wine tasting") in this field. I knew that many countries now made wines that are very drinkable and tasty. If, however, you want to go to the Mecca of Wine, there is really only one place to be. So, after not too much discussion, we decided that France would be our #1 target country.

Next, we needed to pick an area of France in which to live. We had already roamed many of the wonderful regions within the country. In the north, Reims and the Champagne area held a lot of appeal. Reims is a wonderful town with a very nice pedestrian mall in the old part of the city. It also has a cathedral at which a number of my distant ancestors had been crowned King of France. (You had probably already guessed that I had royal blood in my family, right?) We had driven around enough in the Champagne area to know that there were also lots of smaller villages in which we might find an apartment. We were concerned, however, that it might be too far north, and therefore colder than we wanted for the latter part of our stay in November.

Another terrific area we had explored extensively was the Alsace region. Located in northeastern France, it has gone back-and-forth in possession between France and Germany, depending on what country came out on top in the latest war. Because of this, the *maisons* have the kind of half-timbered look that you often see in Germany. And the wines are terrific; one of my favorite wines to drink is a nice dry Alsatian Gewürztraminer. The tasty cuisine of Alsace also has a Germanic flare to it with lots of meats, sauerkraut and potatoes- Yum! Again, however, the northern climate was a concern for us. Alsace might have to wait for a more summer-oriented extended trip.

Provence in the south was also in the mix as was the Côte d'Azur on the Mediterranean coast. We had spent some time in both of these areas several years earlier. They are both beautiful regions with lots of wine to be had. Provence has a kind of beautifully bleak landscape with fields of lavender and hill towns that are stunning. It also boasts some very good wine and is very near to the area of Côte de Rhone wine, one of our favorite French wines. The Cote d'Azur is an area with a tropical climate. And, of course, the appeal of having the ocean nearby is great. The negative to both these areas is the high cost of living there. However, we left them in the mix as possibilities.

Burgundy also held a lot of appeal to us. This area is located in the middle of the country between Dijon to the north and Lyon to the south. It has rolling hills that promote great vine growing for making some superior wines. These same hills provide access to wonderful hiking and scenery. On previous trips we had already visited two of Burgundy's departments- Beaujolais and the Côte d'Or (Golden

Slopes). Both regions have small and medium sized villages scattered throughout with access to larger places if we so desired.

Finally, the Jura Mountain region near the Swiss border was also in the running. We had not spent a lot of time there but had read a lot about it. We had made note of its beauty while watching the three week-long *Tour de France* cycling race on TV. Joni also wanted us to consider Paris. She has an ongoing love affair with the "City of Lights" and everything about it. It is fairly far north but might work if- and it was a *big* "IF"- we could find a place within our budget.

Our list of possible "homes" was now complete- Paris, the Jura Mountains, Burgundy, Beaujolais, Provence and the Côte d'Azur. Didn't eliminate much, did we? We thought about trying to pare it down more but decided instead that we would look at apartments in these regions and see if that, in turn, might narrow our choices for us.

2- Gîte or Bust! (Chip)

I mentioned the Tour de France. This is one of my guilty pleasures and I freely admit it. Bike riders vs. the roads of France! For three weeks every July I look forward to watching *le tour* on television. I will get up very early in the morning to soak up every moment of each stage. My best friends- commentators Phil, Paul (who sadly passed away in 2018), and Bob- are there on the TV to narrate the race for me. The coverage lasts three or more hours each day- heaven on earth!

Now, I can't speak for you but my brain likes to be able to rationalize watching this much TV by doing something "productive." Often it is something like sorting my socks, completing the daily Sudoku, or checking the status of my Tour de France fantasy team members on the Internet. (Yes, I really do have such a team!) Or, as pertains to this book, searching online for *gîtes* (furnished vacation rental apartments) in France.

And this, my friends, is exactly what I did during the summer of 2009. I searched high and low for apartments we might be able to rent. I searched sites in both English and French, sites that marketed other people's apartments or individuals looking to rent their own gîtes. I looked at whole houses, apartments in multi-level complexes, small stand-alone buildings on farms, big cities, tiny villages, in the mountains, on a canal, canal boats themselves... I looked at hundreds of websites. Soon, Joni was getting into the swing of it as well. We became experts at converting rental rates in euros to U.S. dollars.

Although fun, this searching took us well past the end of the bike race in July and deep into the fall and winter. We soon realized we needed a way to keep track of the places we thought would bear further study. Computer folders were made for the regions we had picked as possibilities. Documents were created to allow us to list various properties and their pros and cons.

Around January of 2010 we started going back through possible places. By that time, we had developed a proposed budget and that helped us to eliminate our first region- Paris. It was just too expensive, and we decided it would be too hard to get to know people in such a big city.

After an initial culling, we had shortened a list of about 200 possible homes to around 30 gîtes we wanted to explore further.

To assist us in cutting down our list, we did more internet research. (What did we all do before the internet?) This time we focused on the towns in which the apartments were located and the immediate area around them. Google maps allowed us to actually be able to look up-and-down the streets on which many of them were situated. Some towns were just too small- no stores at all let alone within walking distance. Other apartments did not look like they were in good parts of town. Slowly but surely, we shortened our list.

After numerous such parings, we ended up with a bookmark folder called "Gîtes to Contact." Now Joni put her French language skills to work sending out emails. We had some questions about each apartment that we just could not get answered by looking at websites. She did a great job and we received answers promptly, often in French even though we suspected some of them had great English skills from their websites. These answers allowed us to trim down our list to just six apartments, now called "Gîte Finalists."

For quite some time, we had been associated with a group called the Minnesota Ambassadors of Music, a select high school band and choir that performs in Europe every other summer. We had traveled with them many times and, eventually became the group's Tour Directors. On several occasions, we were able to extend our time in Europe after the students returned to Minnesota. We decided to do the same in the summer of 2010 in order to travel around France and actually look at our short list of gîte finalists.

I am sure some of you might be asking, "Why do you need to look at these places?" I might agree if we had been just planning on staying somewhere for just a week or so. Three months, however, is a whole new ballgame. We wanted to look in every nook and cranny, take lots of pictures, have a face-to-face conversation with the owner(s) and get the lay of the land.

Of our six finalist apartments, two were in the Jura area near Annecy; four others were in the Côte d'Or and relatively close to Beaune. Our studies had shown that both Annecy and Beaune would be nice to be near because they were big enough to have a large selection of stores but manageable enough for easily getting around.

As we were coming from Switzerland, we began in the Jura area. It was a beautiful day, the French Alps were within sight, and we were very excited to finally get an up-close look at the first gîtes. Via emails before we left the United States, we had scheduled to see both places in one afternoon.

We drove into the first small town near Annecy and were pretty impressed. It had several stores and restaurants within walking distance of the apartment. We pulled up to the first address on a quiet street. As we got out of the car and were walking across the street, all hell broke loose. Behind me, I heard a thump and a muffled "Oh my God!" I turned around to see Joni down on the ground bleeding from multiple spots on her face and body. She had tripped on a bump in the road and taken a very bad spill. As I was helping her up and trying to find some Kleenex to stem the flow of blood, I jumped out of my skin as a loud and angry guard dog began barking a few feet from our car. He had appeared on the other side of a gate and he was *not* one bit happy about our presence there.

Next, a shirtless, heavyset man with a cigarette hanging from the side of his mouth came to the gate and started lecturing me in serious-sounding guttural French. I believe he was talking about the dog and not parking in front of his gate. Meanwhile, Joni was whimpering and bleeding on the curbside. She tried to answer him in muffled French while holding a wad of tissues over her face and bleeding lips. The guy finally understood that we had a situation here and called off his dog. Meanwhile he was curiously asking Joni if she was Norwegian. Answering that question was not, at that point, Joni's top priority. He finally reached his neighbor, whose apartment we were going to visit, on the phone. Some semblance of order was restored.

Then things went from bad to worse. Even though, months beforehand, we had made an appointment to see the gîte on this particular day and time, and confirmed it with him in numerous emails, he steadfastly refused us entry into the apartment. Instead he simply wanted to tell us about it. As Joni tried her best lip-bleeding French to coax him into letting us inside, I did my best Peeping Tom imitation at the windows. The landlord never did let us inside. We left feeling very frustrated and, of course, Joni was very sore - both physically and figuratively.

We drove around a while looking for a doctor's office that would check out Joni's face. She had taken some Advil as we left the gîte and finally said she was feeling better. The bleeding had stopped and by that point she was mainly worried about some scratches on her glasses. She was pretty bruised up but game to go on, so we drove to the second apartment. As we drove through the French countryside, we were struck by the beauty of the scenery; rolling hills, rocky bluffs and a lush river valley. Joni was feeling better by the kilometer.

This next gîte was in a much smaller and more remote community. Although a bit farther from Annecy itself, there was a larger town nearby with shopping and a few restaurants. As we drove up to the place, the owner came out with a smile and introduced herself. She could not have been nicer. Noticing immediately that something was wrong with Joni, she offered all kinds of compassion and assistance-towels, ice, a seat. (HEL-LO guy in the aforementioned section above. Duh!) After a brief explanation of what had happened, Joni had made a new friend. The owner was curious about our visit and intent. After Joni explained how long we were expecting to stay on our fall adventure and why we wanted to see her place, she said, "*Mais oui,* you must look closely at a place you wish to call home."

Her gîte was on the second and third floors of their home. They had remodeled this old attic area into a nice two-bedroom apartment with modern bathrooms (Yes, plural!) and an up-to-date kitchen. Huge old wooden beams filled the large combination living room/dining room. It had floor-to-ceiling windows on one wall that looked out over the hills in the distance. In one corner stood a stone fireplace. A deck provided outside seating and eating space. Parking was readily available in the courtyard below just outside our door. It was wonderful and we loved the space. And...Joni didn't fall!

We asked the woman about walking trails in the area and she got very animated. She and her husband were avid hikers and had co-authored a book about hiking in this region. There were many positives to this place and only two drawbacks we could see. One was the lack of any stores in the town itself meaning we would have to drive even to reach a bakery or café. The region was also not a wine growing area. In spite of these limitations, we decided to definitely keep this place in the running. Two gîtes down; four to go.

After lunch it was on to the Côte d'Or area. Joni slept a lot of the way letting her body recover. As I drove closer to Burgundy and the Côte d'Or the fields of vines began to dominate the landscape. We arrived around dinnertime and checked into a bed & breakfast. It was located in a fair-sized town several kilometers from Beaune. In the town center there was a small but thriving business community. The reason we were staying in this particular B&B was that they also owned one of the gîtes in which we were interested.

After a good night's sleep, Joni was feeling much better. We started our day by visiting our third apartment finalist in a neighboring small town. The owners met us at the agreed time and were very nice. They showed us around and let us really take our time, as they understood that this was a long-term commitment for us. The building was very old but, like many such gîtes, had been remodeled. It was a nice place but, for some reason, just did not strike a chord with us as a three-month home.

We then drove to Beaune itself to look at a place there. Beaune is a bigger town but has an old center that is very charming. The apartment was just a few blocks from this area. This one was a former tannery, now converted into vacation living space. Once again, it was in an older building and did not have a great floor plan. We were not as impressed with the kitchen and bathroom as we had been at some other places. And, was it just my imagination of could I still smell hides that were once drying hung from the hooks in the ceiling? We withheld judgment, however, until visiting our last two finalists.

The next day, we began by visiting the gîte attached to the B&B at which we were staying. We had high hopes for it because we had found the B&B itself to be very nice and we really liked the owners. This apartment did have some charm. It was on two floors. The lower level was the kitchen, dining and living area; upstairs was a bedroom and bathroom. The couch in the living room folded out to make a second bed if needed. Although the location was nice and we liked the owners, it was smaller than it had looked in its website picture. That left one more place to visit.

After lunch, we drove down the road to the final gîte on our list. It was literally within the walled courtyard of an centuries-old complex. It not only held the apartment in which we were interested but also the family's living quarters, and another larger gîte as well. Best of all it was a working vineyard. We met Karine, the wife of the owner, and she showed us around the place. She was warm, informative and friendly. She did, however, want to know more about us before we became her next-door neighbors for three months. Understandable. Joni and Karine had an immediate connection and Joni thought, "She'll be my first friend in our French home."

We entered the apartment through an old door that looked like it had been made in the middle ages. Up a flight of circular stone stairs, worn by centuries of people tromping up and down them, was the apartment. Like the previous place we had seen, it was on two floors. A large living space dominated the first level. It had a floor-to-ceiling fireplace on one wall and a table long enough to seat ten. A small but well-equipped kitchen (dishwasher- wow!) rounded out that level. Up the open staircase we went to find two bedrooms with a sink room in each. Between the bedrooms were two smaller rooms- a toilet room and a shower area. Although not as close to the village center as the previous apartment, it had much more charm and space. Later that day, I walked and timed out that it was only a five or six-minute hike to the downtown.

That evening, over a long dinner and some good wine, we talked at length and re-examined all the apartments we had seen, listing their pros and cons. It did not take us long to figure out that we had found our new "home" in France. Even after some serious reflection, the final apartment we had seen at the winery came out on top. On our way out of town the next day, we drove back and told them we would sign up for an extended stay the following fall.

A major hurdle in our adventure had been overcome. We were super pumped to have this yearlong quest come to fruition.

Part Two- Bon Voyage

3- Arrival, Shock and Birthday (Joni)

One year later, after my final year of teaching, a retirement party, and our summer in Minnesota, fall arrived and we finally departed for our big adventure in France. We didn't travel light- we had three full-sized suitcases as well as two smaller roller bags and two backpacks. We packed swimsuits and we packed mittens. Umbrellas, raincoats, sweatshirts and shorts. Measuring cups, music speakers, medications and maps. We hoped we had remembered everything we needed. We were finally off on our grand adventure.

We arrived in Paris, picked up the Peugeot that we were leasing, and off we went to Fontainebleau- a medium-sized town about an hour from Paris. We were able to check in early to our hotel, have dinner, and crash, catching up on some much-needed sleep.

The next day, after breakfast and checking out of the hotel, we began our drive to Burgundy. We arrived in our small village on a sunny afternoon and drove to the apartment we had carefully selected the previous year.

Have you ever met someone briefly, and thought to yourself, "I could be friends with that person if we got to know each other better"? That is what I thought to myself last summer when Madame Karine Michaud showed us this apartment. I was looking forward to seeing it- and her- again.

On the day of our arrival it was her son, Christian, who showed us in. He said that his father would be home soon. When I asked about his mother, he looked at me with steady but sad eyes, saying, *"Ma mère est morte."* ("My mother is dead.") I gasped at what he said. Even with the language barrier, Chip realized something was very wrong. Christian went on to explain that his mother had passed away the previous November of cancer- only three months after we met her. I grieve the loss of a friendship that will not be.

The shocking news sapped some of the emotional high out of our arrival day. We unpacked, went to eat a light dinner, and spent our first night in our apartment.

Our first night in our apartment, I had trouble getting to sleep. After years of imagining myself in France as I nodded off to sleep, I didn't know what I should be visualizing anymore. I was finally living in France!

The following morning, we finally met the patriarch of the Michaud family, Antoine. The vineyard had been in his family for hundreds of years- as in, since before the French revolution. Karine and he, however, had only recently had the property restored and made into their family home. As extra income they also built in two apartments to rent out as vacation rentals. This first encounter with Antoine was a bit intimidating- I found his French to be difficult to understand, and he clearly felt the same way about mine! He didn't speak a word of English, so it was sink or swim with this guy, which, of course, turned out to be very good for me and my French language skills. It was Sunday morning, and he looked surprised that I didn't realize that all stores in town would be closed, as well as most restaurants. Oh, and by the way, the same holds true for Monday. This was a lesson that it took us a long time to master- in France, family comes before profit. Plan ahead. Antoine did let us know what restaurants were open and which ones he recommended. He then went back to work in his office, and we were off to be fending for ourselves.

Two very friendly members of the family soon learned to greet us as old friends every time we entered the courtyard of the property. They were the two beautiful dogs who lived there. I was thrilled to have two canine companions. We were instructed to never let them into our apartment, but we are guessing that not all guests have followed this rule, as we sometimes heard one of the dogs settling in just outside our door, especially if we had been cooking.

We soon discovered, by the way, that son Christian lived in his own "bachelor pad"- a small apartment on the property. He worked at the winery alongside his father. Christian had attended a very specialized high school in the area, where the main course of study was winemaking. Only in France. Although we didn't meet her right away, we soon learned that Christian had a special friend who sometimes came to stay. We'd see a new car arrive in the parking area on Friday evenings, and a lovely young woman would hop out. She would nod in our direction if we happened to be nearby, and we slowly put two and two together as to why this woman seemed to be hanging out more and more. Finally, Chip went up to her and introduced himself. From then on, she greeted us with a smile and we gradually got to know Madeleine, Christian's *petite amie*.

There was one more member of the Michaud family left to meet, and we met her a few days after our arrival. This was Anne, daughter of Karine and Antoine. Between the time when we met Madame Michaud and the time when she passed, Anne was married. It must have been such a happy day for both mother and daughter, in spite of knowing that their time together was drawing to a close. Now Anne was living nearby with her husband, and she was expecting her first child. What a lovely gift to this family- new life. It reminded me of my own experience, after my father passed away at the age of 64, just six weeks after my marriage. Before long, I became pregnant. Now that I am a grandmother myself, I realize how much that new life meant to my family, not just to me and my husband.

The next day was my birthday. In the morning we had the grand adventure of grocery shopping in a *supermarché* for the first time. We really felt like fish out of water. We could not find anything. As an example, milk was not in the dairy section because it is not refrigerated and is disguised in ordinary looking boxes, more like macaroni and cheese than a carton of milk. I can't imagine how confused we must have seemed, staring at a package of food forever, trying to decide what it was and if we should try it. It took us over two hours to buy what would have taken twenty minutes in Minnesota. It could only get easier.

In the afternoon, as part of my birthday celebration, we drove to another village and had a tour of a factory that makes Crème de Cassis (black current liqueur). This liqueur is mixed with white wine to make the drink called "Kir". (More on this in a later chapter.)

We concluded my birthday by dining in the best restaurant in town. It was expensive, but the food was fabulous. I had roast turkey with a mushroom sauce; Chip had pig cheeks. That would be the cheeks on the pig's face, not at the other end. They were delicious. And we drank a toast in memory of Karine.

As we dined, we realized that we had survived our first couple of days in France- driving, grocery shopping, my birthday, Cassis and a huge loss. We had begun finding our way around our adopted village, and were getting to know our apartment. We heard the church bells every morning and every evening. We had arrived.

4- Our Town and Family, or "Getting to know you..." (Chip)

We began to get acquainted with our adopted hometown. There are really two villages in one. The first is the old town that backs right up to the side of the hill and into the vines. This is where many of the wine makers and sellers live. The other newer village has grown up very nearby on flatter land by the highway and rail-line that run through the valley. This latter section contains new housing developments, a *crémant* factory (sparkling wine), a couple of car repair garages, restaurants, some wine tasting rooms (what else?), a barrel-making factory and the town's new sports complex. The winery where our *gîte* was located was in the old village.

Soon after our arrival and getting settled in, we decided to take the first of many walks through the town. As we turned out of the apartment's courtyard and began to stroll towards the heart of the village we ran across a peculiarity to villages that are hundreds of years old- the buildings and roads came first; sidewalks were an afterthought. And, since the roads were originally only wide enough for carts pulled by workhorses, it did not leave much room for human traffic. Sidewalks are often shaped like the teeth of a saw; wide then narrowing to about a one-brick-width before jutting out again. Or sometimes they just disappear altogether. As we walked, little white cargo vans, extra tall vine tractors, and cars whizzed by us. The roads also curve and change widths themselves. Thus, we noted to ourselves, it was not necessary to always walk next to each other around here. A line of two often worked much better.

After a couple of blocks, we turned onto a smaller road. Much more peaceful. We were struck by the rustic beauty of the place. Old stonework and stucco walls dominated the landscape. On the stucco buildings just enough of the plaster had fallen off here and there to give them an ancient aura without looking run-down. It looked like we had just stepped into any generic World War II movie. The shooting could start at any minute. I was sure a German staff car would come driving through with half-lidded head lamps.

Walls surrounded each home with gates leading into courtyards. As we walked, we saw signage posted outside a number of gates- *Vigneron* and *Viticulture* (both meaning "wine-maker")- and wondered at the sheer number of wine makers located within this small town.

We were jolted of our *rêverie* by loud barking. Two dogs were taking it very personally that we were walking by *their* gate. They looked hungry. Luckily, the gate was made of sturdy iron and kept them from their prey. A few yards later, after our hearts had stopped racing, the same event occurred at another gate. *Mon Dieu!* These dogs were devious. They would wait until we were directly next to their gate to start up. During our stay, we walked this same block many times and received the identical treatment on each pass. No matter which direction we went, the first two dogs would always alert the other two to be ready for our passing.

Another right turn and we were out of dog-attack range. We passed over one of the several streams that flow out of the nearby hills and through the town. A choice was given- cross the stream on the road or take the footbridge on the side. The footbridge's rusty color and see-through flooring gave us pause so we stuck to the road.

We were now on the *Rue d'Ecole* (School Street). Continuing on, we passed the local elementary school. Kids were playing in the schoolyard for recess. We both looked at each other and smiled. Even though they were just elementary students, the same thought passed through both our brains- it was good to be a retired teacher! Of note was that even the school courtyard had some grapevines planted in it. Could they be for the teachers' personal use after really rough days?

The rising road passed between two fields of walled vines nestled within the town itself. We later learned that the local vintners consider these walled areas, named *clos*, special. They believe that the extra heat collected in the limestone walls assists the grapes to ripen more quickly. Not much space was dedicated to grassy yards in this town.

Almost magically, the town transitioned from houses and vines to the downtown business area. It probably took you longer to read this than it actually took us to walk the entire way. Having been in many small French towns, I can say that this town square was one of the most idyllic I had seen. The downtown was *très* picturesque and right out of a movie set. (In fact, it *was* once the set for a movie.) Three main roads and several smaller ones converged onto *le centre-ville*. Two buildings dominated the central area: the church with its tall steeple, and the beautiful *hôtel de ville* (town hall). In the center of the area, a fountain recognized the town's main industry of winemaking happily bubbled. Three small hotels faced the plaza, each with their own restaurant, bar and seating on the sidewalks. A *tabac* also had tables and chairs under the plane trees near the fountain. Several of the locals sat there, drinking coffee, smoking and reading the paper. We caused only the briefest of passing interest as we entered the area.

Interspersed between the hotels were the many businesses and services that drew us to this town to begin with: *boulangerie/patisserie* (bakery/ pastry shop), *charcuterie/boucherie* (deli/butcher), a pharmacy, three banks, a small grocery store, two *coiffeurs* (hairdressers), a tourist office, a realtor, a florist, the post office, and- of course- several wine shops offering tastings of the local wines. Shuttered windows on the floors above the stores had boxes of red geraniums. Except for the hotels, these upper floors held apartments.

Past the village church was the *Place de la République*. In France, you soon learn that each town has such a place set aside to honor its war dead from the two World Wars. A monument there listed the names of those who had died serving their country. It was a somber reminder of how much these wars impacted the country.

Across from the *Place de la République* was the local post office. Good to know.

We noticed a large bronze plaque on the wall next to the post office door. Closer inspection revealed that it was placed there to recognize Thomas Jefferson's friendship with France. During his time in France in the late 18th Century, Jefferson toured extensively in the Côte d'Or and loved these villages and their wines. He purchased a lot of Burgundian wine that was eventually shipped to his home of Monticello in Virginia. In 2010 the French erected plaques throughout the area celebrating Jefferson. This is just one example of French appreciation for their connections with the United States, and the friendship the two nations have enjoyed since our country's inception.

Signage in France is not like in the United States. They don't put up multiple billboards pointing you in the correct direction. The signs are subtler and sometimes are hidden altogether. At roundabouts, they have signs pointing towards the major city of each exit's direction. Do not, however, expect to find a sign that actually states the highway numbers; you have to know the names of the cities in the direction you want to go. The French don't waste a lot of paint refreshing signs either. I guess the philosophy is, once everybody knows where something is, why do we need a sign?

Leaving downtown by another road, we had seen a sign for the *bibliothèque* (library). One day, after doing our shopping, we headed down the street to find it. We passed more vintners, houses and *châteaux*. We reached the end of the road. No library. Hmmm. Perhaps we just missed it. Several more times, Joni attempted to find the library, always turning out of the downtown onto the road with the sign. She carefully walked the street taking care to look at all the buildings and signs. Finally giving up, she asked someone where the library was. He told her to go down the road with the library sign and then turn right at the building that said "Parking Spaces" on it. She dutifully walked the road again, this time turning where she was told. A small driveway curved to the left into a courtyard of a recently remodeled area with parking. She investigated each door and finally found one with a small piece of paper taped to it with the library hours. Eureka! No sign, however, anywhere on the street side of the building indicating the library was in this particular courtyard.

While we were wandering around this same courtyard we heard a trumpet being played. On closer inspection, we found that a trumpet lesson was going on in another part of the building and a clarinet lesson in another room. Again, carefully checking the doorways, we found out that (drum roll) our village had a music school. This was quite exciting news to a couple of retired band directors. (Note- no sign *anywhere* in town about this, either.)

Now that we had found it, we did make our way back to the library when it was open. It was not large, but it had a good variety of fiction and non-fiction, as well as children's books. A very kind woman named Suzanne helped Joni sign up for a library card. She also helped me find some easier children's books and graphic novels that I could read to improve my French vocabulary.

Hearing us speaking English, the woman began to speak English to us. She was quite good. She had a friendly face and a warm smile. Little did Joni know that this woman was to become a lifelong friend. After a brief conversation at the library, Suzanne knew that we were staying in town for three months, that we were Americans, and that Joni wanted to improve her French. Suzanne suggested that they get together once in a while to practice speaking English and French together. From that point on, they would go for walks two or three times each week, speaking French for thirty minutes, and then, for Suzanne, speaking English for another half hour. During these *promenades*, they discovered similar beliefs, and they solved many of the world's problems.

The most interesting example of unique signage appeared on the road from Beaune to our village. We often would drive by a small sign that read *hôpital* (hospital). I said to Joni, "In all the reading I have done about this town I didn't run across the fact that it had a hospital." We decided that this indeed would be a good thing to find. Later that week, we were talking with Anne at the *gîte*. Her husband is a doctor. Joni asked her, "Does he work at the hospital here in town?" She responded "*Non*" with a puzzled look on her face.

Several weeks went by. Occasionally I took a different road into or out of town hoping to spot the elusive hospital with no luck. Finally, I decided to resort to the internet. After a few futile searches I finally found it. The sign did not refer to a modern hospital with all the bells-and-whistles we might need. Instead it referred to a leper hospital whose ruins existed near the highway. It had been an offshoot of the famous *Hospice de Beaune*. We had driven right by its ruins on many occasions with no idea that they were what the sign referred to. Luckily, we got through our stay without needing major medical attention.

Over the months that we lived in our village, we walked almost every road in town- many more than once. Coming from a major metropolitan area in Minnesota where we had to drive to everything, it never got old for us to be able to walk to the downtown and the local stores. We began to recognize and greet people we met on the street. We saw familiar cars and dutifully waved back to the drivers. The storeowners and Monday night pizza-truck ladies greeted us with smiles.

Only the guard dogs never cut us a break.

5- All Things Cassis (Chip)

One Sunday, we took a drive over to a couple of towns we had not yet visited in the Côte d'Or. The rolling countryside around Burgundy provided us with super views of the vines and manicured pastures with the white beef cattle (*Charolais*) that are raised around these parts. At one point, Joni started humming a melody from Beethoven's Pastoral Symphony.

While I was driving home and Joni was napping in the passenger seat (too much wine tasting?) I reflected back on dinner the previous evening. We ate at a small restaurant that was new to us. Although we did eat at home most evenings, on weekends we tended to eat out more often than not. And to treat ourselves, we often have an *apéritif* called a *Kir*. This tasty drink is made using *Aligoté*, a Burgundy white wine, mixed with a little something called *Crème de Cassis* or just called Cassis.

Early in our stay, as we were exploring the area, we kept seeing signs for a place called *Cassisium*. (No, I'm not making that name up.) The place was a combination theme-park attraction/factory tour/Cassis tasting room. After you've done lots of tasting and are on your way out, you have to walk through the store where you can buy all types of Cassis.

We decided to spring for the English language guided tour and were lumped onto a tour with a group of twenty-year-old students from Holland. They were studying the hotel/restaurant/bar management business. Many of them looked like they had managed to study a little too much at the bar the previous evening. As we progressed through the factory, the guide tried her best to engage them in a question/ answer quiz about Cassis. Mostly what happened was that the students socialized while their teachers kept saying, "Shhhh!" in a loud whisper. (Ah, so thankful to be out of the teaching business. We could just smile at what was going on.)

Near the end of the tour we were ushered into a small theater. The lights darkened and a disembodied cartoon Cassis berry popped up on the screen. He humorously lectured us about the history and process of making Cassis.

If the kids had been paying attention they would have learned that Cassis is a very sweet dark-red liquor made from Blackcurrants. Blackcurrants are similar to our Gooseberries in North America. The drink was first made in the Dijon region of France in the 16th century. The juice from the currants was collected in much the same way as grape juice for wine except the crushed currants were combined with sugar. Lots of sugar. The juice was fermented in large tanks, followed by oak barrels. The Cassis was then aged in various ways to make it stronger, or combined with other liquors to make a wide variety of drinks. As with wine, the French turned this into big business with many varying degrees of *Crème de Cassis* quality control. You can get regular Cassis, SuperCassis, SuperDuperCassis, etc.

I have my own theory on why it was made. Centuries ago the peasants were looking for anything that they could make into a fermented alcohol drink either for themselves or to sell to the nobility. Better- and safer- than drinking the water in those days.

As we reached the end of the tour many of the students perked up considerably when we reached the sampling room. A few, however, were looking mighty green at the sight of more liquor. Others of them were still "tasting" when we had called it quits. And well they could, because there were roughly thirty varieties of Cassis-flavored liquors being poured.

Many of the drinks made with Cassis contain the word *Kir.* Felix Kir was a resistance fighter who fought against the Germans during WWII. He later became Mayor of Dijon. His favorite drink was something called a *blanc-cassis* (white wine mixed with Cassis). The press picked up on this and began referring to his drink as a *Kir* to slur his name. Not being shy about his drinking habits or his ego, the mayor encouraged the name (can you imagine a better campaign idea?) and was re-elected four times until his death.

Enough of the history lesson; let's get back to the drinking! We already know that a *Kir* is *Aligoté* wine and *Crème de Cassis*. In the United States they still call the drink a *Kir* even if they just use any white wine they have on hand. The proportions are one-part Cassis to two-parts white wine. If you have SuperCassis, its one-part Cassis to four-parts white wine. Of course, these recipes can be varied to taste, and that in itself makes a fun game.

A *Kir Royale* is Crème de Cassis mixed with Champagne from the Reims region of France. (Pssst. Any sparkling wine will do but don't tell the French that.) A *Téméraire* is made by combining Cassis with *Crémant*, a sparkling white wine made in Burgundy. *Téméraire* translates as "reckless" in English. Do you think this has to do with someone who drinks too many of these?

A *Kir Breton* or *Kir Normand* originated in the northwest of France. It mixes *Crème de Cassis* with Apple Cider made in the Brittany and Normandy regions.

A *Communard* or *Cardinal* mixes together Cassis and RED wine. Joni had one of these at dinner one evening. Upon being questioned by this reporter, our waitress explained to us that a *Cardinal* uses the proportions of one-part Cassis and ten-parts red wine. She then came back with two wine glasses filled part way with water- "This one represents one-part Cassis and this one represents ten-parts wine." I guess she really wanted us to get it correct. Later in the evening, she told us that, at a recent dinner in another nearby village, she had ordered a *Rouge Gorge* (Red Robin). This drink was made with *Crème de Cassis, Crème de Mûre* (Blackberry Liquor), red wine...and gin. Another road trip was brewing in my mind. The research would have to continue.

On another restaurant menu we noticed a drink called a *Sweet Blush*. When questioned, our waiter told us it was made with vodka, citric concentrate, cranberry & raspberry juices and *Crème de Cassis!* Ah, the possibilities are endless...

6- Back to School (Joni)

As was mentioned in a previous chapter, to get to the town center we walked past the public school. The small school is built with large sliding glass doors in each classroom, which open onto the asphalt play area in front of the building. In the warm days of September, these doors were frequently wide open.

Chip and I didn't argue very often on our trip, but we did argue about whether or not school was in session as we would take our near-daily trek into the heart of town. Although the doors were wide open, we could hear nothing. There was no noise coming from this primary school, filled with children ages 6 to 10. Was it a day off for the students? Chip frequently insisted that this was the case. I'd shake my head "no" and say, "This is France." I had been told by a French friend that no parent would ever say, "Have fun in school today!" as their child rushed out the door in the morning. "Work hard." or "Behave yourself." would be a morning reminder, but the concepts of school and fun are mutually exclusive.

I'm not saying that children in France don't have behavior problems, but it is so rare that you see problems in public, you almost think that this could be the case. Actually, you hardly see children out and about in public without their parents. We would, from time to time, see high school aged people out with friends on Friday nights. Other than that, a student walking along the streets of a French town meant that school just got out and they were walking home.

When we went to a concert of Renaissance music one evening, a group of twenty or so middle school kids came into the concert space. Chip and I looked at each other and shook our heads, both thinking the same thing: "Great. These kids are going to ruin the concert for us." We were seated a few rows back from the kids, and they were perfect audience members, much better than many adults would be back home.

Wanting to immerse myself in the French experience, I thought it would be fun to be a volunteer at the school. I imagined myself coming in once or twice a week to help students with their English studies, their music lessons, or even just to help with filing or hanging up displays. Much to my surprise, this concept does not exist in France. There is no such thing as a "parent volunteer." In France (and I suspect in all of Europe), "parent involvement" means something very different from what it means in the USA. In the States, "parent involvement" often means being that dreaded "helicopter parent" who is über-involved in every aspect of their child's life, protecting the little darling from ever getting a scratch, or, heaven forbid, a "B+". In France, parent involvement means looking at their child's "*cahier d'école*" (school notebook) every evening to see what the child needs to be working on at home, and to see what comments the teacher might have sent for the parents to see. This is so ingrained into the French culture that a teacher can write a note to a parent telling them how horrid the child was that day, and the notebook will actually get home- without that page torn out- and will be shown to the parent. Parent involvement in France means staying on top of the child's studies and homework.

I digress. One of my French teachers at the Alliance Française in Minnesota warned me that the volunteer concept didn't exist in French schools, so she wrote me a letter of introduction, with suggestions of how the school could possibly make use of my skills.

I took the letter to the school, and...couldn't figure out where the entrance was. There was no sign announcing "Main Entrance", much less the standard notice reminding folks that, "All visitors must sign in at the main office." Luckily for me, some children were out on the playground (meaning, flat asphalt play area with no playground equipment of any sort). They were very excited to greet a visitor, and showed me where the entrance was.

Once inside, I realized there was no office at all: no secretary, no principal, no nothing except for classrooms. I asked the children how I could find the principal, and they took me to a classroom where I met Mr. H, a charming young man in jeans and a t-shirt. He was not the principal, but he was the "head teacher" of the school. I showed him my letter, and he seemed happy to read it. He knew of another school that had an American working there for an entire school year. He took my letter, then told me that he would send it to the head principal in a larger area town, and would get back to me.

Each small town in the area has its own primary school, regardless of size. For example, in another smaller village nearby there is only one teacher for their school, much like our one-room schoolhouses of days gone by. At approximately age 11 the students will be bused to a larger town to attend middle school (I say "approximately" because it is much more common for a student to repeat a grade in France than in the USA). Since what is taught is completely dictated by a national curriculum, a teacher in a one-room school must be a very busy person, preparing materials for each grade level every day. In our adopted village, a school of approximately 70 students, there are three classes, each with a mix of two grades in it.

After leaving the public school, I walked down to the private school in town. The gate was closed, but there was a buzzer, so I rang it. And rang it. I walked around the entire building, once again impressed by how a school could be so quiet. I got up the nerve to open the gate, and went to the door. Knowing now that there may well be nothing but classrooms, I hesitated to knock, but eventually I resorted to that. Still no response, and the door was locked. Dejected, I left the building, closing the gate behind me. As luck would have it, a townswoman was walking by, so I asked her how to get into the building. She looked at me puzzled, and then explained, "Wait until tomorrow. Today is Wednesday." And this is how I learned that the private church-run schools are closed all day on Wednesdays.

I never went back to the private school, imagining myself busily working at the public school on a regular basis. After ten days or so, I heard back from Mr. H, and he said that the school was very happy to invite me to come. What they wanted was a presentation to the students about the differences between American schools and French schools, as well as information about how we celebrate holidays in America.

Yikes! Instead of being busy volunteering at school, I was now busy preparing a presentation. I know that it is difficult to understand young children at times in one's own language, so I was very concerned about understanding these children in French. After all, a five-year-old would most likely have a more diverse French vocabulary than mine, sad to say. The thing that worried me more than that, however, was that they might not be able to understand *me*. Adults don't have a problem with my American accent (in fact, for some reason, they tend to think that I am German, Dutch or Norwegian). But as adults, we know to compensate for a mispronounced 'r' or 'th' coming from someone who is speaking their second language. Children would probably not be so forgiving.

I practiced and practiced my script. A French friend helped me to express myself in more typically spoken French instead of the French I knew from textbooks. Chip helped me put together a PowerPoint presentation with a few pictures from home as well as a map of Minnesota. The night before my school visit, I had a tough time sleeping. This volunteering idea had taken a new course, and I wasn't sure I was ready for it.

I arrived at school at 1:30 on the day of my visit which is during lunch break. This was to give me a half hour to get set up before the students arrived back at school at 2:00. In France, students (and their teachers) have a two-hour lunch break every day, and most of them go home. This lunch break, by the way, means that the children are in school until 5:00 pm. When I would walk past the school near noon, I would always see mothers waiting outside for their child to be dismissed for the noon meal. For children who have both parents working outside the home, there is a lunchroom, which is separate from the school. I am told that there is some pressure on the women who work for the family winemaking business. These women often do the record keeping as well as wine tastings for visitors, but they feel like they are looked down upon if they don't bring their children home for lunch. But I again digress.

Mr. H. took me to the library of the school, which was a classroom with books. It was much smaller than what I was used to seeing in an American "media center." A little past two o'clock, the first, and youngest, group filed in (they were in lines in the hallway). These students were ages six and seven. They sat down on the floor and were a charming audience. Showing the use of the French language in Minnesota ("Etoile du Nord" on our state flag, Lake Mille Lacs, Lac Qui Parle) was totally unimpressive to them. Of course! They see French every day, so it seemed quite normal to them that we would see it, too. However, when they saw the map of the school where I used to teach, a school that housed more students (1600) than was the population of their town, they were impressed. And when they saw that there was a swimming pool in the school, they went crazy. Who ever heard of such a thing?

When I told the students that at my school, the students and staff had only twenty-five minutes for lunch, and that nobody left the building, they thought they had misunderstood. Culturally, this just didn't make sense to them. Why would anyone want to eat that fast? I didn't have the heart to tell them that for American students, much of that time is spent waiting in line.

It really got their attention when we started talking about holidays. I showed them a picture of children in costumes, and of a Jack-O'-Lantern, and they had heard about this. But when I told them about Thanksgiving, and that we eat pumpkin pie, they lost control. "You don't eat pumpkin in a pie! That's for soup!" they told me, as if I were the biggest idiot on earth. Well, at least I knew they were understanding me!

Then we moved on to Christmas, and I showed them a picture of my granddaughter and me standing in front of our Christmas tree. The point was for them to see the tree. One little girl in the front exclaimed,

"*Regardez! Je vois la tour Eiffel!*" (Look! I see the Eiffel Tower!) Oh, dear, I must be misunderstanding her, I thought. She repeated herself. Sure enough, she was right. There, hanging on our tree, was an Eiffel Tower ornament purchased on a previous trip to France.

As if seeing this famous Paris landmark weren't enough, what really got the attention of the students was something to which, as a Minnesotan, I hadn't given a second thought. Out the windows in the picture you could see lots and lots of snow. More snow than any of them had ever seen. More than any of them probably ever *will* see! Minnesota received more than twenty inches of the white stuff that December alone, so it looked impressive.

Each class departed by calmly getting in line, and then the next group arrived in the same way. After three such presentations, I was done, relieved, and feeling pretty good about things. As I was leaving via the playground, children ran up to me and asked me if I knew various playground games, which I may have if I had known what the names of the games meant. Having these young ones gather around me to ask more questions was a true highlight, knowing that I had made some sort of connection with them in spite of our cultural- and verbal- differences. From time to time after that I would see a child look at me a little too long in the grocery store or post office (always with *Maman* or *Papa*) and I would smile at them, knowing that I must have met them at the school. Or it could have been my French!

7- Making Wine 101 (Chip)

At home, I dabble with my winemaking hobby in our basement with some modest success.

You might think it odd that a person who prides himself on his Wisconsin heritage- Swiss/German, Badgers, Packers, brats, beer!- would now have such a love affair with wine. Actually, it took a long time for me to get to the point where I truly appreciated wine.

My beer drinking days had a huge head start. My mom would go so far as to give me sips of her beer when I was growing up. I remember these small tastes as being deliciously unlike anything I had ever tasted before. As a true child of the Badger State, it left me wanting more.

When I first traveled to Europe, I was overwhelmed with what could be done with beer. I tasted colors and varieties we never had in Wisconsin. Upon returning home, I began looking for some of them in the liquor stores. I found them, but what a price tag! As a poor beginning teacher with a young family these beers were just not in the cards for me except as a special treat. An option presented itself when I was turned on to beer making by another member of a bagpipe band in which I was then playing. (Yes, I played in a bagpipe band; no, you will not hear that story in this book.) These kits provided me with the tastes I was missing from Europe.

Years passed. I acquired certain physical ailments that required me to be more careful about my carbohydrate and calorie intake. Beer was high in both of these and suddenly became a *non-non* in my diet. Enter Joni and her love of wine. I began trying it more often and, as my palate adjusted, I really began to enjoy the intricacies of the tastes involved. I had a whole new world of wines to explore and learn about.

A while back, when I was first discovering the joys of wine drinking, we visited a small vineyard in central Wisconsin. After a genial tour and enjoyable tasting with our host, Patrick, we sat on his shady veranda sharing a glass of his Gewürztraminer. I told him that I wanted to start making some wine myself but did not know how to get started. He retreated to a room in his house, brought back a spare Wine Expert catalog he had around, and talked to me about how he had started. He covered the equipment I would need, recommended wines to begin with, bottling, early pitfalls I might encounter, etc. Generally, he encouraged me to give it a try. His parting advice: follow the directions until you know what you are doing, and sanitize, sanitize, sanitize.

Now, several years later, I have made many a bottle of wine, mostly to the delight of family and friends. Via this process I have a far better understanding of what goes into making wine and a much greater appreciation for those folks who make really good wines for a living. Hence, you might imagine that, when I heard they were in the early stages of making this year's vintage at the winery, I was quite excited.

Antoine, the owner and wine-maker, had told Joni that we could observe the process. He owns several good-sized plots of vines scattered around the Côte d'Or. He primarily grows two grape varieties for which this area is known: Pinot Noir for red wine and Chardonnay for white wine. Antoine, along with his son/able assistant Christian, makes a number of fine wines, some that are considered to be *Premier Cru.* That is some very, very good wine.

When we arose one morning, we looked out the apartment's front window to the courtyard below. We were greeted by an army of oak wine barrels being prepared for the filling process. A gas heater had been fired up to create steam. The barrels were put hole-side down on a device. Once turned on, it then shot hot steam up into them. This served to clean the barrels and to swell the wood, thus resealing them as much as possible.

We strolled through the courtyard to one of the workshops across from our apartment and looked onto quite a scene. In a large room, several very giant tanks filled one whole wall. They contained wine juice in its primary fermentation phase. What would become red wine (now called the *must*) still had the grape stems and skins in them to give added color to those wines. Christian was in one of the huge vats full of crushed red grapes shoveling out the remains. It was put into a big drum-like device called a press. Using an air-filled bladder, this machine slowly spun around and pressed the remaining juice out of the red grapes. Eventually only the skins were left behind and none of the valuable juice. Standing in the large vat, only Christian's head and shoulders were visible above the edge. He gave us a big grin and shouted "*Bonjour!*" We did not notice anything peculiar about him at the time, but he did seem to be in a very friendly mood.

We smiled back, said "Hi", and then started talking to Juliette, a young woman who, as it turned out, became a very good friend of ours. The daughter of another local wine maker, she was currently working for Antoine. As it turned out, she also owned vines and was quite an accomplished vintner herself, but more on that in a later chapter. Juliette and Christian were good friends who had studied wine making at a local high school dedicated to this particular craft.

Juliette told us that the grapes had been picked in early September, shortly before our arrival. After a first pressing, the *must* had since been sitting in these large vats undergoing its primary fermentation process that converts the sugar in the grape juice to alcohol. Occasionally the vintners must punch down and break up the *must* as well as the thick cap that forms on it called *pomace*. This is the head that develops on the juice during the rapid first fermentation. The smell in the room seemed like it alone would be enough to get you drunk- very heady and yeasty.

Juliette let us taste some of the wine in this early stage and told us it was *très jeune*- very young. Even so, it already tasted like it would make some fine wine. I asked Juliette about whether they added yeasts to the juice to get the fermentation started as I did with my wines at home. She said they did add a small amount but that this varies from vineyard to vineyard with some vintners just depending on the natural yeasts in the air.

After a while Christian, still in the giant vat, said something in French that I did not catch. Juliette reached up and handed him a towel. She then turned to us, smiled and said, "*Christian est tout nu.*" (Christian is totally nude!?!?!) No wonder he was grinning ear to ear when we walked into the room. He later explained that shoveling out the vats is a very messy process and the juice just ruined any clothing that might be worn. To prevent this, he shoveled the vats out while naked. We decided to leave and give Christian a little privacy.

Depending on the variety being made, the young wine was eventually transferred to another vat or it was taken across the courtyard where the barrels were being prepared. After each barrel was filled, a plug called a *bung* was driven into the hole. Filled barrels were then stacked in one of the *caveaux* under the various buildings on the property. These ancient basement-like areas had rounded stone ceilings. Because they are mostly underground the temperature is consistently between 55° to 60° F. This temperature, along with a constant humidity, is what vintners want for aging wine. The barrels were stabilized using wooden blocks. There they would sit for a year or more undergoing a secondary fermentation, aging and clarifying.

At this point in the year, the employees had other tasks to complete around the vineyard. After the harvest, dead or diseased vines had to be drilled out of the rocky ground and replaced with new stock. When we hiked in the vineyards at this time of the year, we saw little white cargo vans amongst the vines almost magically appearing like mushrooms that popped up overnight. Workers would drive out and spend their days at this task. We could always tell when this was going on because of the columns of white smoke rising from the side of the roads where they were burning dead vines.

Around November, when the sap had stopped flowing in the vines, the pruning operation began. You might think this mindless work but it is not. A great deal of planning must go into how much to prune off of the vines on a yearly basis. Take off too much and it will not produce enough grapes the following year. Leave too much on and the vine spends too much energy producing leaves and not enough on grapes. A Burgundian *vigneron* wants to get enough grapes from each vine for two bottles of wine or enough for one bottle of the best- *Grand Cru.* Generally speaking the pruners were to leave two stems for production the following year. All this pruning was done by hand. Depending on the size of the vineyard's acreage and the number of workers involved, the process might take one to two months of time.

During the winter, the vintners, especially those who owned small to mid-sized operations, would go about marketing their own wine. They set up and provide tastings for local purchasing clients, attend wine shows in other towns where their wine can be tasted and purchased, and regularly submit samples of their product to the government-run labs for testing.

Throughout the spring and summer the vines must be watched over and tended to. Sometimes if too much foliage grows on the vines, they drive a peculiar looking tractor through the vines to trim off extra leaves. This vehicle looks vaguely like tractors in the Midwest, but they seem to be up on stilts so that the body is raised enough that they can drive right over a row of vines to trim them.

In late summer, the grapes are tested more frequently for sugar content, acidity, etc.

In August, just before the harvest begins, the wine that was barreled the previous fall needs to be bottled. Bottles, corks and labels are ordered up. After the wine is bottled it is stored in more cave space under the chateau for up to three more years before it is sold.

Then, in early September, this whole process starts again with a new harvest.

Antoine's vineyard is relatively modest in size for Burgundy and yet I could not believe how much grape juice was moved around the chateau during the several weeks it took to complete the barreling process. Enough barrels were filled with juice to make 25,000+ bottles of wine. Of course, this was going on in numerous facilities (aka "homes") within our small village. All you have to do is walk around the town at this time of the year and the smell of fermenting grapes will waft over you. And this place is just one of many such villages within the Burgundy area, and there are many such wine making areas throughout the country. Multiply it all out and the experts will tell you that France produces seven to eight billion bottles of wine per year. Incredible! *Magnifique!*

8- A Cave, a Race...and Frogs (Joni)

In an earlier chapter Chip wrote about our love for *Le Tour de France* bike race. As we were planning our first fall in France, we thought it would be exciting to experience the excitement of a bike race in person and not on television.

To that end, one Saturday we headed out towards the city of Tours in the Loire Valley. Most people visit there to see the wonderful castles of the area. We went to be at the finish line of the last professional cycling race of the season.

On our way to Tours we stopped at the Caves d'Arcy-Sur-Cure and took a guided tour of one of the caves, which boasted the second oldest cave drawings in the world. We walked approximately the length of two football fields back into the darkness. The tour was only in French, and the guide spoke very quickly, so to say something was lost in translation would be an understatement. However, we were able to be very close up to some of the prehistoric drawings, which are estimated to be 28,000 years old. There were no glass panels over the drawings, and really, anybody could have gone right up to them and touched them. There were no photographs allowed, however. There are more than 170 drawings in this cave alone. In the 1970s, a cleaning was done with acid, and about 80% of the drawings were, unfortunately, damaged. Still, it was fascinating to think about how our ancient ancestors got enough light back in the place to create these works of art. Why they put them way back in the depths of the cave will most likely never be known.

We rely heavily on our GPS in Europe, but "she" failed us miserably when driving to our hotel in Tours. The city was building a new rapid transit system, and there was an ever-changing schedule of detours, depending on the day. Even the locals were frustrated by daily surprises due to road closures. Since the GPS didn't know about this little snafu, we just kept going in circles, not realizing that the hotel was only a half block away from us at some points. Finally, I called the hotel, and the very kind woman there stayed on the phone with me as we navigated through the busy traffic and detours. "Where are you now?" "We just went past a shoe store." "Good, let me know when you get to the corner with a used bookstore." And on it went for twenty minutes. She and I were speaking French, I was giving Chip instructions in English, and all the while the GPS was babbling away, having a hissy fit because we weren't following her instructions. Somehow, we did get there in one piece, and I ran into the lobby and gave this complete stranger a kiss on each cheek. Perhaps I was becoming a little bit French?

Tours is a very beautiful city, with public gardens, large boulevards, museums, an enormous cathedral, fountains and a large neo-renaissance *Hôtel de Ville* (city hall) which looks quite Parisian. More on that building later.

On Sunday morning there was a large flea market, so we strolled through that and bought a few trinkets. By 1:00 pm we wandered back to the street where the bike race would end and had staked out our spot immediately across from the winner's podium, just a few feet from the finish line.

For me, especially, it was an afternoon of "Mind over Bladder" since we couldn't possibly leave our front row spots and get them back. For anything.

At 3:30 they started projecting the race on a big screen, and we listened to a one-man commentary on a microphone for all of us. This amazing man did not come up for air until after the awards ceremony- he spoke with the speed of a horse race announcer for nearly two hours! This same announcer also announces for the Tour de France so we had heard his voice when we watched that race on television at home.

The winners crossed the finish line around 4:45. The race was not as exciting as it might have been because the leaders were ahead by 90 seconds for the last 50 kilometers (90 seconds is an eternity in bike racing.), and as the *peloton* raced by us it was such a blur that we couldn't tell one rider from another. (Yes, Chip and I are avid enough fans of the sport that we recognize the faces of the stars when we see them on TV.) The three cyclists who placed in the top three were unknown to us- good for them!

We did, however, see one very familiar face on the stage with the winners. Minneapolis and Tours are sister cities, and the Minneapolis mayor was there on stage, applauding along with everyone else at the appropriate times, as if he understood what was being said. Who am I to say he didn't? I doubt that the people of Minneapolis knew that he was in France on this particular week. The City Council back home was having discussions about budget cuts for city services while *Monsieur le Maire* was enjoying the good life in France.

It was really a kick seeing this event in person, including all of the media, cameras, official vehicles, etc. The trip was well worth it.

We had a copy of the local newspaper from the day and noticed a small ad that invited supporters of the race to share in a glass of champagne at the *Hôtel de Ville* after the race. Well, we thought, WE supported the race, didn't we?

After a most urgent stop at *la toilette,* we decided to see what this was all about, never really thinking we could get in. However, it was an event that was clearly open to the public. The building was even more opulent inside than out. We climbed marble stairs to the second floor, past statues and a monument to war heroes. We entered a long room with a high ceiling, featuring floor to ceiling windows, more statues, and an elaborately painted ceiling in the style of the Sistine Chapel. There were free glasses of champagne as well as snacks and cookies. These were laid out on long banquet tables as if we were visiting royalty. Staff made sure that the bubbly was available, and that snack trays were replenished. We fit right in with all of the townspeople- in jeans and t-shirts- who presumably enjoyed this tradition annually.

After dinner on our second night in Tours I ordered a dessert called "*Pain Perdu*". That would translate as "lost bread". I had no idea what it might be, but I had to find out. Well, now I know where the term "French toast" comes from because that's what this was: warm salted caramel sauce on the grilled bread, and a warm fruit compote on the side. I've been told that Pain Perdu is a dessert you might have at grandmother's house, a last-minute dessert you can throw together in a hurry when you have nothing else on hand. All I know is that it was wonderful, with a little taste of home in every bite.

We love driving the back roads of France through small villages, stopping at weekend "*marchés aux puces*" (flea markets) and simply watching for the surprises that seem to await us around every bend in the road. On our drive back to our village from Tours, we decided to take such a route.

On the side of a quiet country road we found a small and inviting restaurant for a lunch stop. It was called "*La Grenouille*"- The Frog. Do you think a restaurant would have a chance of success in the USA with that name? The building had a large golden frog hanging above the entrance outside. Inside, there were frogs everywhere- paintings, statues, flower pots, and stuffed animals. Heavy wooden tables stood before a wood-burning fireplace keeping the patrons warm on a cool fall day.

I ate some of the best fish I've ever had in my life in this cozy, quirky place. I decided to say "*non*" to the many options of frog legs on the menu. Before we left, I of course made my usual pit stop in the lady's room. The toilet seat was green, with a painting of a frog's face on the seat cover. The toilet paper was held in the hands of a smiling green frog, and even the wastebasket was covered with painted frogs.

Without the frogs, this little place would have earned five stars in the "rustic charm" category. With them, well, it was truly memorable, and great finale to our weekend adventure.

9- Making Wine 102 (Chip)

On several occasions I was given the opportunity to assist Christian and Juliette with their daily wine tasks around the vineyard. I happily took them up on their offers. Being a former band director who was used to the set schedule of the school day, I asked Christian what time I should meet them in the morning. He said something to the effect that when they got started would be a good time. Hmmm. Not exactly the answer this Type-A guy was looking for.

Most days I would rise early, drink coffee, have breakfast, catch up on some email, read my book and get ready for the day. On the days I would get to help with the wine, I would watch the courtyard out the window from our apartment and hope to catch a glimpse of Christian so I would know when to head out. Another clue I had was when I saw Juliette's old white Renault vehicle pull into the parking area behind our *gîte*. I knew then that it would be about time to go to work.

On one occasion I was assigned to stir the wine that had been put into the barrels a few weeks earlier. This operation mixed the lees (dregs at the bottom of the barrel) back up into the wine to promote more fermentation. Juliette showed me how to take the bung (barrel plug) out of the barrel and use one of the stirring sticks to mix the wine. There was a long rod and another that was slightly shorter with a strange curve to it. "Why two such sticks?" I wondered. I quickly learned the reason. The barrels were stacked in two levels. The upper level is so close to the curved ceiling in the cave that only the shorter stick with the curve would go into the barrel hole and down into it. At home

I accomplished this same stirring process using a plastic rod and my electric drill. I told this to Christian and he just laughed at me. "No electric drills used here." he said.

This was the second time I had wondered about some of the tools they used. Another time I was asked to stencil numbers onto the barrels so they could track samples taken from each barrel. I was given a set of old rubber stamps that looked like they might have been the first ones ever made. When I told him that some of the barrels already had numbers on them he gave me a wooden handled scraper that looked like it belonged in a museum. It may have looked old but it worked great to scrape the old numbers from the barrel lids.

After stirring a barrel I would add wine of the same type from a holding tank to top off the barrel. This was necessary because there was some natural leakage and evaporation from each barrel. This lost amount of wine is often called "The Angel's Share." The process was then completed by wiping down the barrel with a solution of water and a very small amount of sulphite. This cleaned any contaminates from around the hole. Finally, I reinserted the bung into the hole and, *voilà*-done. A fairly simple and easy task, but I was thrilled to be involved with it. Until I started counting up just how many barrels there were in this one cave alone.

As I was working on my assigned task, my mind, as it tends to do, wandered. I wondered more about these strange items called wine barrels. Certainly they must have run out of oak in France after all these centuries of wine making. And how long did one of these barrels last?

Located in the Burgundy village of Saint-Romain was one of the area's barrel-making factories, *Tonnellerie François Frères*. These days they make dozens of barrels in an hour. Hydraulics, power saws and other modern equipment now make the whole process fast and efficient, but it is still very much a hands-on operation. If you ever find yourself in Burgundy, it is fun to stop here and watch for a few minutes. There is a handy glass door right at the edge of the parking lot for viewing.

The huge stacks of wood being aged outside the barrel factory told me they wouldn't be running out of oak any time soon. They covered acres of land. Not only did they use oak from forested areas within France, they also imported it from a number of other eastern European countries. One of France's oak forests is near the Vosges Mountains where numerous battles took place during World War I. The oak from this area was not used for many years after the war because the metal shrapnel in many of the trees would ruin saws being used on them.

On our travels to visit various vineyards in the Côte d'Or, I often asked about how long they used a single barrel. The variety of answers surprised me. One friend, Samuel, who makes a very high-end wine in older, more traditional ways, only uses each barrel once. He then sells them off to other vintners and buys new ones. Other makers use barrels for up to seven or eight years or longer. The average seems to be around three to four years. After that, most vintners sell their used barrels to whiskey makers or to other less-picky vineyards. After a few more years, these barrels are cut in half and end up as planters at your local home improvement store.

Depending on the quality of the wood used and the size, a typical French wine barrel costs between 500-800 Euros each. That is about $650-$1000 each. They are shipped throughout the world for use by wineries. On a recent trip to New Zealand, we were doing some tasting in the Otago Valley wine region. At one of the vineyards, they were using an old barrel as a tasting table. As I was sipping my wine I looked at the barrel and, sure enough, it had been made in the very village where we had been living the previous fall.

More on barrels and barrel making in a later chapter.

One day when I had finished my wine-stirring task, the vineyard owner, Antoine, asked if I would like to accompany Juliette into Beaune to drop off wine samples at the lab. My first thought was, "They have a lab to test wine?" During the car ride, Juliette explained that every wine produced in France must be tested periodically in government labs to see that it meets certain criteria.

After circumnavigating most of Beaune, we pulled up in front of a modern three-story office building that in the US would have housed dentists, accountants and up-and-coming lawyers. This one, however, contained the government wine laboratory and other wine-related businesses.

While Juliette was depositing the most recent samples with the receptionist, a nice woman came out of her office and asked me if I would like to look around the lab facilities- at least I believe that is what she said in French. Juliette said something to her about my limited French skills but she waved me on anyway. The woman chatted her way through several impressive looking labs, complete with technicians in white coats, test tubes, bubbling pots, incubators, etc. As she talked I picked up a few words- *sucre, acidité, alcool* (sugar, acidity, alcohol). I did a lot of nodding and smiling. She seemed very proud of her labs. We finally circled back to the reception area. After several *Merci beaucoups,* Juliette and I were on our way back to the vineyard.

Juliette told me that one of the other functions of the building we visited was to offer classes in various aspects of wine making and tasting. She explained that there were actually several schools in the Beaune area that were only for people going into the wine business, even at the high school level. If I had taught in a school like that I might never have retired.

Most, if not all, of what the public sees about the French winemaking process is all very romantic- caves, wine-stained barrels, old tools hung on walls, ancient wooden wine presses- all in buildings that look like they were made when Charlemagne was alive. In this day and age, however, it is big business and highly regulated. The visit to the wine lab and learning about the wine schools was one of those "Hmmm" moments for me. How does this jive with the old stirring sticks or scraper I used on the barrels earlier in the day? I believe it is this: The French wine makers take great pride in the history of their family vineyards. Although they are willing to embrace modern conveniences such as tractors, labs or bottling machines, they have not lost sight of the fact that they are making a product that has long-established traditions and they take pride in the romantic history that wine plays in their society. This is why they hang on to some of the old tools and still do some tasks by hand as their ancestors did. The end result? Fine wine made with great pride that we can all enjoy.

10- Timeout for Oktoberfest (Joni)

Oktoberfest in Munich. If you have never been there, you probably have a visual image of what it might be like. If so, I am here to tell you that you are wrong. If you think it is big, it is bigger. If you think there is an excess of beer drinking going on, well, "excess" isn't really a strong enough word. The size and scope of this event really are beyond description.

We made the drive from Burgundy to Munich via the infamous autobahn. Just to make life a little more interesting, there was plenty of road construction, causing lanes to shift and narrow. In spite of the construction, I still managed to get the speedometer up to 180 kilometers per hour (112 miles per hour). We were very happy to arrive at our hotel in one piece! We had an obligatory dinner at the Hofbräuhaus, and turned in. The next morning we did some sightseeing in this beautiful city. Then, after a nap at our hotel we set out for the park where the action takes place.

We arrived around 5:00 p.m. Entry into the festival is free. The setting is huge. It feels much like the Midway at the Minnesota State Fair, except on steroids. There are fourteen "tents" (they are actually buildings) which are each run by a brewery- Löwenbräu, Paulaner, Hofbräuhaus, Spaten, etc. Each tent holds thousands of people. If you want reserved seats in a tent you need to order your tickets a year in advance. Otherwise, you can come in and try to find an empty seat.

The huge park also has lots of carnival rides, games of "skill" (such as throwing bean bags at targets), vendors selling not only Oktoberfest memorabilia and souvenirs, but pretzels, roasted and spiced nuts, bratwurst, fish. Nothing, however, on a stick *à la* the Minnesota State Fair.

I expected to see some people in lederhosen and dirndl dresses. I would say that about two-thirds of the men were either in some sort of leather shorts or pants, or at least were in traditional checkered shirts (including Chip). Almost all of the women were in dirndl dresses-knee length, mid-calf or ankle length. Some of them were absolutely beautiful. Others? Well, a few of the women in dirndls worked hard at trying to look non-traditional. They had very short skirts, wore high heels or knee-high boots, fishnet stockings, and showed abundant displays of cleavage. And not just the *young* ladies. Oktoberfest has it all. I did NOT buy a dirndl, but I did buy a women's version of a plaid shirt. I sort of looked like I was on my way to a hoedown, but I did my best in the situation.

We had tickets for the Hofbräuhaus tent. The tent holds about 10,000 people and was decorated with huge hanging hops plants. It was really beautiful! We were seated up on the balcony with our friends Jürgen and Renate from Dusseldorf, and our friends Chuck and Julie from Minnesota. Julie's parents were also with us.

The balcony was perfect for us. We could go down to the main floor, walk around and see the band, and experience the controlled chaos there. After a brief foray, we were able to escape back to our table. The downstairs was packed with lots of younger people who I'm sure were feeling pretty awful the next day. It is a good thing that Munich has great public transportation.

I'm not saying that our area was calm and sedate. Anything but that. For instance, there was a gentleman who frequently stood on his head on his table and kicked his feet around in the air to the music. People (yours truly included) were standing on the benches to get a better look, or to get into the music. We had two young ladies at our table (German) in their dirndls who were planning to spend the night sleeping in their car, as there were no hotel rooms to be had for miles. They told us that it was very common for people to come to Oktoberfest and sleep in their cars. I'm not sure that helps with the hangovers the next morning!

The evening started out with a large polka band, but later in the evening that changed to a rock band/electric folk music group. The crowd really got into "Sweet Caroline", "Hey, Baby", and "Bohemian Rhapsody", but when they played "YMCA", my friend Julie and I jumped up on the bench to do the hand motions, while hundreds of puzzled Germans watched our table with confused expressions on their faces.

Although the Germans were not familiar with our YMCA antics, they were well acquainted with another song which we Americans had never heard. It started out as a quiet ballad about a neighbor named "Alice." When the song got to the chorus, however, thousands of beer-filled Europeans sang along to the heart-warming refrain, "Alice! Who the F-—is Alice?" I assure you they did not just shout the first initial of that four-letter word. The chorus returned several times in the song, and the crowd shouted along gleefully each time.

The waitresses were just what you might imagine. Sturdy women in their dirndls, able to carry eight full one-liter sized beer mugs at a time all night long. You could only get the beer made by the brewery of the tent and only in one-liter mugs.

We began our dinner with beer (duh) and appetizer trays. In true German fashion, the trays were huge, with various sausages, cheeses, radishes, pretzels, sliced onions and shaved horseradish. A couple of hours later we got our dinners. Each dinner had, among other things, half of a chicken. Just a nice light meal- with no utensils to slow us down (clearly, we weren't in France anymore). Really, it all tasted great. We left around 9:30 p.m. in order to return to our hotel via public transportation. It was now dark outside and many more people crowded the park between the giant tents. Although a few were quite loud, most folks were just having a good time. And a few looked like they were turning green.

After getting back to our hotel we went to sleep immediately and slept soundly through the night. The next morning our friends reported that around 2:00 a.m. a very vocal group returned to the hotel and were loudly singing drinking songs. Instead of calling the police, all the other German guests shouted out their windows for them to be quiet and go to bed. They did. Amazing.

11- Hiking- Côte d'Or Style (Chip)

There are simply no two ways around it- I love to hike. This was not always the case. When I was growing up we would often go camping. My mom or uncle would want us all to go on a hike. It was not my idea of a good time. I would have far preferred to hang around the campfire, swim in the lake, or read my latest "Hardy Boys" book. Hikes to me always seemed like forced activities. Wasn't the point of a "vacation" to do what you wanted to do?

A few years ago, my doctor became quite concerned with my rising blood sugar levels. It was apparent to him and myself that, if something did not change about my lifestyle, I would soon become a full-blown diabetic. Changes in diet and exercise had to ensue. I had started running several times during my adulthood but my asthma always made aerobic exercise difficult for me. And living in Minnesota where the cold weather was not conducive to running a good part of the year didn't help. Fortunately, I had started seeing a terrific asthma doctor. He got me on some new medications and inhalers that allowed me to exercise with better results.

In Minnesota, we live close to a major trail created out of an abandoned railway line. I decided my exercise routine would be walking. I started with 20 minute a day, and was soon doing 30 minutes without any problem. I began to feel that something was naggingly wrong with my day if I did *not* walk. My walk time continued to increase towards an hour a day. At the same time, I began looking for more varied places to walk. I created a number of loops within our neighborhood. I checked out parks and nature reserves in the area. When the outdoor temperatures dropped, I would go to the local mall and do the rats-in-the-maze walking with other retirees.

As the days and months passed I kept walking and began enjoying it more and more.

Fast-forward several years. I have now purchased Nordic hiking poles and am wearing out several good pairs of New Balance shoes per year. As Joni and I looked for a place to spend an extending living period in Europe, I was always looking at the hiking possibilities.

Voilà, la Côte d'Or! Rolling hills transition from vineyards to woods and back again. Toss in an occasional farm sporting white cows in idyllic pastures and small picturesque villages spaced a few kilometers apart. For someone accustomed to the flatlands of the Twin Cities it was like stepping into hiking nirvana for me.

Another advantage to the Côte d'Or is the proximity of the hiking. In Burgundy I had a wide variety of hiking places right outside of our village or just a very short drive away. I'm sure Burgundy is not the only place in the world with these conditions, but it seemed great to me.

I'm sure there are some folks who would say, "Chip, you're crazy! Why stop at the Côte d'Or and its puny hills? Go to the Alps, man!" Yes, I have hiked in the Alps and there are many wonderful climbing and hiking areas with staggering views of snow-capped peaks. These are wonderful areas for daylong hikes, or hiking and camping. However, there are a few drawbacks. One is the climate. For me, I was looking for an area where I could hike much later into the fall without much more than a sweatshirt. In the Alps there is already snow early in the fall. Côte d'Or high temps in the fall are in the 50s and 60s, with no signs of snow.

I'm a map-person. Wherever I travel, I like to have detailed maps so I can get oriented. A number of years ago, before the existence of a GPS or a Smart Phone with maps, Joni and I were driving through an area of Germany known as the Romantic Road. By the end of this trying day, however, there was little feeling of romance for us! We learned a new German word: *Umleitung*, or detour. After being directed off of the road on which we wanted to travel, we never saw another sign of where to go for the detour. Our trusty AAA map from the travel agency back home was called "Germany & Surrounding Countries" – not the most detailed once you were off the main roads.

After driving around for an hour or so we arrived in a town of which we had never heard. We pulled into a station for a fill up. While Joni was visiting the lady's room ("Go when you can; not when you have to."), I was trying to get directions to the town we were heading for from the attendant without much success. Finally, I asked if he had any maps for sale. He took me to a shelf full of various maps of Germany. I was in heaven. By the time Joni got back to the counter, I had purchased the thickest, most detailed map book of Germany it was possible to get. Nothing but the best, as I was sick of getting lost. Of course, it weighed about 100 pounds but I was not really thinking about my suitcase for the flight home just then. And I did feel a gentle breeze in the car because Joni was constantly flipping pages every couple of kilometers as we were cruising down the autobahn.

In the Burgundy area, I acquired a bundle of maps- Burgundy, Côte d'Or, various cities and parks, and...most importantly...a hiking map. I had actually purchased it the summer before our grand adventure when we were checking out rental apartments. During the winter in

Minnesota I would get it out on occasion and peruse it- looking at the hikes, the distances, the geography, et al. I was ready to hit the ground running, err...hiking.

A couple of days after our arrival, we loaded the Nordic hiking poles into the rental car and headed for a nearby trailhead. There we found another map of the trail mounted on a pole. All seemed straightforward, so off we went.

As we headed up the trail we were chattering away. I was sort of half-paying attention to the trail, believing it was clearly labeled. I had read all about the use of yellow markings on the map I had. Silly me. Little did I know that the people who marked the trail did not use special poles driven into the ground with little yellow signs saying, "Tourists, go this way!" Instead, little splotches of yellow paint are on a tree trunk or stump, a telephone poll, a monument, a statue, or maybe a stone bench. Over the course of many such hikes we had even seen yellow paint on rock somewhere in the path, or on a dumpster outside of the city hall. They are always at different heights, but at least they are always small. By the faintness of some of these markings, they seemed to have been applied shortly after the French Revolution. I knew I was going to have to learn some French for this trip but I did not know I was also going to have to learn to read "Trail" as well.

After getting ourselves truly lost, we worked our way back to a main path. While I was trying to decipher the hieroglyphics on the rocks and trees, we heard some noises approaching. I turned to Joni and said, "Someone is coming on horses." Just then two people came up the path. In French, Joni asked them if they could show us where we were on my hiking map. The man said, "Yes, but it would be easier to do in English." We found out how to get back to our car, thanked them and off they went down the trail. Joni to Chip: "I guess those weren't horses; they were Dutch." So, you get the picture- as with most things, there is a learning curve to finding these little yellow hiking symbols. Once you figure it out it's amazing how your mind adapts. Now we notice these little yellow markings even when we are not hiking.

Eventually I branched out from the marked trails and created my own hikes to take. Some days I was very surprised by what I came across. On one occasion I was walking in the woods from one town to another. The trail took me alongside a stream. Suddenly, looming out of the woods, the remains of a very old stone building appeared. It looked like it had once been a mill but now it was in the middle of nowhere. It was wonderfully picturesque in its dilapidated way with the trees growing up through where the roof had once been.

On other hikes I have found smaller things- old gnarled pieces of dead grape vines, antlers, Geckos, snails, wild cats...and two Dutch people. Several times on hot fall days I have been going uphill and asking myself, "Why didn't I pick a different way today?" only to be rewarded at the top by a terrific view out over valleys with hills beyond, and at times a hazy outline of the Alps far in the distance.

One October Sunday I knew hunting season was in progress so I decided to stick to the roads between villages. As I was climbing one such road to hopefully get a great view of the castle at *la Rochpot*, I heard a horn echoing off the distant hills. At first, I was surprised because no one honks car horns here. Then I heard it again but this time with a distinctive jump in pitch. That was when it hit me- they're using these horns in the hunt. I heard several of them being played throughout that morning walk and the dogs barking as well. It sort of gave me an idea of what it must have been like when the Burgundian Barons of the past were out doing their hunting.

After several very foggy days in the village, we decided to go for a hike in a nearby section of the region that we had not yet explored. As we drove through the winding roads and neared our destination, the sun suddenly broke out and we had a wonderful hike on a late fall day. We climbed through the pastures, past the cows, through the woods and, in the middle of nowhere, came upon the ruins of the *Abbaye Sainte-Marguerite.* Sitting in a clearing, this abbey was built in the 11th century by the monks of St. Augustine. It thrived until the end of the 16th century when it fell into decline. Now in ruins, the walls of the abbey's church continue to rise through the trees. With the sun streaking down it was a pretty picture of life gone by.

We have met some wonderful folks on the trail and in the towns we pass through. Once while taking the trail through a sleepy little burg, a woman came out onto her deck because her dog had been barking at us. She had a couple of empty wine bottles in her hands. We said hello and she responded in kind. Then, with a big smile on her face, she said, "Don't worry, I have not been drinking by myself!"

On another hike one late Saturday afternoon, we randomly stopped at a vineyard to request a tasting. Answering the door was Bérénice, the wife of vintner Arthur. We explained that we were interested in trying some of their wine. She immediately broke away from what she was doing which was getting ready for a dinner party that evening for 20+ people. She took us down into their cave.

Chattering away enthusiastically, her energy and enthusiasm for their product was apparent. Nothing fancy or prestigious about this tasting room; it served one purpose- evaluating the wines. Once we ascertained that she had more important matters to get back to, we cut our tasting short, but promised to come again.

Before we left Bérénice took Joni by the hand and said, "You have to come and see what I'm preparing for tonight." She hauled Joni into the house to show her the dinner table with its multiple place settings and the food she was making. As they were going into the house, she turned back to me and rattled off some French so fast there was no possible way I could pick up a word of it, so I just smiled. Then she turned to Joni and said in French, "Men! They are never interested in these things."

We have since been back to visit Arthur and Bérénice several times with friends, and to taste and buy more wine. They simply could not be nicer yet very proud (and justifiably so) of their wines.

Using walking poles in rural France is not common. Late in the fall, on a cloudy and cool day, I had been out for a long walk. As I was strolling back into our village using my Nordic poles, I decided to sit down on a bench in the town plaza to relax for a couple of minutes. One of the locals walked by me and asked, "(Several French words) *ski* (more French words) *la neige est dans les Alpes?* I think he was asking me, "Don't you know the snow is in the Alps?" I smiled and, as he walked on, he laughed at his own joke. You know that laugh- a very guttural and nasally "*Hunn, hunn, hunn, hunnnnnn!*"

One day just before lunchtime I departed the *gîte* for a hike. It had been raining on and off much of the morning but seemed to be letting up so off I went. Christian, knowing my penchant for hiking, had shown me a spot where he loves to go. Among his many sporting activities, he is an avid rock climber. He directed me to a path that would take me to one of his favorite spots. Following his directions, I drove to the next valley west to a spot near a small village. Parking the car on a roadside, I hiked up a dirt road and then left onto a narrow path through the woods.

After almost an hour of climbing through the woods, I heard the screeches of falcons launching out of the tops of the pine trees near me. I could see that the trees were thinning in the direction I was hiking, and a minute or so later, I emerged to one awesome view! I was high on the edge of the rocky cliffs above the town. I could see way down the length of a valley to two other small villages and, far in the distance, the larger town of Nolay. Fields of vines clung to the lower sides of the valley. Pastures where white *Charolais* cattle grazed were just below the tree line across the way. The falcons soared and hunted out over the cliffs. The sky was dotted with small rain clouds alternating with blue sky and sun, giving the entire scene a mottled and surreal effect. I sat on the rocks, ate my lunch, and just soaked it all in. It was one of those moments I'm sure we all have had when you realize that no camera can possibly capture this view, and that life just doesn't get any better than this.

12- Days in the Cote d'Or (Chip)

From time to time we have had folks ask, "What do you do with all your time in France?" Just like at home, most days are spent on fairly mundane things like buying groceries, catching up on emails, reading, etc. Occasionally, we strike out to see or try something new. Here are some examples of what can happen at these times.

One day as we were walking back to our apartment from the *centre ville*, we noticed a relatively new wine tasting room that had opened. We decided to go in and take a quick look around. Inside, a cheery voice greeted us, and asked if we would like to taste some wine. *Pourquoi pas?* As she poured wine for us, we began talking with her. Her name was Camille and she had just recently moved to this village. As I may have mentioned before, Joni has a knack of getting anyone, even new acquaintances, to tell her their life stories. So, as we tasted wine, Joni and Camille talked and became fast friends.

Camille grew up in the Beaujolais wine area in southern Burgundy. She was very interested in making her way in the world of wine. With her knowledge of wines, her outgoing personality and her command of English, we felt certain that she could succeed. We all agreed that we would see each other again for more wine tastings when our friends from the United States came to town. Not only did we see Camille many times for these tastings, but we socialized with her on several occasions.

Fast-forward a number of years. Camille has now married, and we have met and gotten to know her husband, Maurice, an accomplished free-lance photographer. She now helps wineries promote and export their products.

On and off over the years, Camille had voiced her desire to experience an American Thanksgiving. We all finally agreed that they would travel to Minnesota the following fall to enjoy Thanksgiving with our families. We had a great time immersing them in all the holiday's traditions, as well as showing them around some of our state. We were happy to get to reciprocate their hospitality in France. And Camille brought lots of really good wine.

Joni and I had decided that we wanted to take a short road trip to visit another nearby village we had heard about. We love to do this type of activity. We usually pick a destination or two, but the fun of such a day is discovering the places and things you happen across along the way.

Semur-en-Auxois is a town we had driven by on a number of occasions but had never stopped to visit. It had some interesting features we had seen from the highway. The Auxois River runs through the northern part of the Côte d'Or and is connected, via canals, to the Sâone River in the south. It is a major waterway in this part of the country. Therefore, many towns have sprung up along it. In the middle age days of yore, they were fortified and served as toll collection stations.

We parked near the Tourist Information (TI) office and made it our first stop. The helpful young man gave us a *plan de ville* and some directions for a walk we might like to take around the town. As we started down the first street we passed under a double-walled city gate. In the middle ages, the gate had been used to keep the city safe and to control the flow of travelers (like us!) into the city. We looked at where the drawbridges had been hung and at the holes for pouring boiling oil down on the heads of the unwelcome.

We had a nice stroll around town dodging short periods of rainfall by visiting whatever little shop we might be passing at the moment. Pictures were taken and some gift shopping was accomplished.

After lunch (with hot chocolate!) at an outdoor café, we did the standard drill prior to departure. The rule is "Go when you can; not when you have to!" I trooped off to *la toilette* first. Anyone who has traveled in Europe knows that this can sometimes be an adventure. We have often said that we should take pictures of all the various bathroom configurations and equipment we run across on a trip to Europe. It would make a very interesting...and different...coffee table book.

A door in the rear corner had the "WC" sign for which I was looking. I entered a small room no bigger than a broom closet. There I found a urinal and the world's tiniest sink. Honestly, one hand would not even fit into it. Directly across from the entrance there were two stalls-one with a picture of a gentleman complete with top hat and tails; the other a shapely *mademoiselle* on the door. Some quick deduction told me which one to use. Before I go further in this story, let me say that I could have just used the urinal that was located in the larger part of the room ("larger" being a relative word here). Although I have become more accustomed to French public bathrooms I wasn't that sure I wanted some unknown woman to walk in while I was relieving myself, so...the stall it was. I open the door onto an area that barely held a small toilet. I entered and turned around to lock the door. The backs of my legs were touching the toilet seat and my knees were rammed into the door. I was wondering how I was to get myself turned around to relieve myself. Instead, I just lowered my pants and sat down. It was at that moment that I realized that the other stall was already occupied. Yes, by a woman. I waited until she finished up, washed her hands in *la petite* sink and exited. All too weird by American standards but quite the norm in rural France!

After completing my business, I tried to pull up my pants while standing up at the same time. My head bonked into the coat hanger on the back of the door. I checked for blood, and then gingerly exited the stall. After washing my hands, I got to experience the other great mystery of French public bathrooms. Why do they install electric hand driers that are so low-powered that it would take half-an-hour to dry your hands? So that you still have to be in there when the next person enters?

After Joni got the delight of experiencing the WC, we were off to our next stop of the day. She had heard that the church in the nearby town of Saint-Thibault had recently had an exterior face-lift. Twenty minutes later we were staring at it. The stone and sculptures had been cleaned of centuries of pollution and shone a brilliant white. Joni had read that the money for the work had been raised by the sale of artwork. An English painter had made the village his new home, and he donated the proceeds from some of his work.

As long as we were there, we decided to also take a quick tour of the small interior that was under restoration. Behind the altar I happened onto the tomb of a knight named *Guy de Thil*. According to the church records, he had made a donation to found this priory in 1190. A beautiful and peaceful three-dimensional representation of him lay on top of his tomb. It was carved from red marble. He was dressed in his chain-mail armor, and his long sword rested under one arm and down the side of his leg. A serene look was frozen on his face and his hands were forever locked in a praying position. Two small angels rested by his shoulders. Shafts of dust-filled sunlight were passing through the window and down on his final resting place. This beautiful and unique tomb was one of those "finds" that you just happen upon but remember forever.

As mentioned in a previous chapter, we like to take hikes when we are out and about in the area. On one such outing we ended our hike in a small village. We had seen signs in the town for the "Boutique de Bacchus" and had been wondering what this was. We noticed the store front on our way back into town and decided to pop in for a visit. We were oohing and aahing over the wonderful stone coasters and other creations in the store. Suddenly a voice from the back room says, "Is that Minnesotan I hear being spoken?" Out comes one of the co-owners, David. It turned out that he had moved from Minnesota to France a number of years ago and started up a business of printing vineyard labels on stone coasters, cutting boards, and other items. It was a big success.

We introduced ourselves, told him our story, and several purchases were made. As it turned out we had several mutual acquaintances back in Minnesota. During our conversation, we found out that David was also friends with Antoine, the owner of our vineyard apartment, and he was also quite a wine connoisseur himself. Although he would not brag about it, we discovered that he had actually been inducted into the *Confrérie des Chevaliers du Tastevin*, a prestigious group of wine "knights" located in the Côte d'Or. Quite an honor! We agreed to stay in touch during our time in the area. After the typically long Minnesota good-bye, we wondered at the coincidence of finding another Minnesotan in this *petite ville* in the French countryside.

We planned badly and found ourselves without food for dinner one Sunday night. We decided to drive into Beaune to eat at a place called the "Buffalo Grill". We had noticed this chain or restaurants in France on previous trips, and we were craving some American-style burgers and fries. Blasphemy, I know.

As we approached the restaurant, the Country & Western music was blaring. The place would be considered very politically incorrect in the USA. There were statues of Native Americans (cigar store Indians), buffalo skins on the walls, and totem poles on the sides of the doors. There was a mounted buffalo head over the bar. The menus had pictures of cowboys. Excerpts from classic western movies were playing on the TV screen. Before dinner we were brought a small bowl of popcorn. How American- don't we always get served popcorn at dinner?

The burgers were OK, but the fries were great as they always seem to be in France. However, in the land of the best bread in the world, the French still haven't figured out how to make a hamburger bun that doesn't self-destruct and break into little pieces. Maybe we weren't supposed to pick them up, but cut them with a fork and knife? After five weeks of chocolate mousse, crème brulée and all sorts of other wonderful desserts, we enjoyed sharing a brownie with ice cream on top.

We have written before about the lack of clear signage. This came into play on another afternoon when we were on the road to nearby town. As we looked at the map we found two other features we thought we had time to visit. One had a "Roman Ruins" icon by it on the map. It was romantically called *Fontaine Gallo-Romaine*. Off we went to see the Gallo-Roman fountain; that should be cool! I was imagining a picturesque basin with sculptured levels rising out of it like the Trevi Fountain. Water would be cascading down over muscular horses and partially clad women. It wasn't...even there. After driving around the small town in which it was supposed to be located we finally resorted to asking for directions. We were told it was in the cemetery of a small chapel in some nearby woods. After driving down a small path we were halted by a gate. We walked to the church and found the fountain. Not quite what I expected. It was just a hole-in-the-ground that had an old-looking stone cap perched over its top. Ah well...in my mind it will always be the fountain I expected.

The other sight we hoped to see was an old windmill called *Moulin à Vent*. We drove up a road that looked like it was last used by the Romans who made the fountain. After winding around, we emerged on top of a treeless hill and saw...five huge, brand new wind turbines whirling away as they generated electricity. This can't be what they meant on the map?!?! We drove to the nearest town and looked around. That took all of two minutes. I saw a small toy windmill located in someone's yard and told Joni I'd found the *Moulin à Vent*. For some reason, she failed to see the humor in this.

Nearby, two men were working on an old car in a garage. Joni rolled down her window and asked them where the windmill was. One said,

"The windmill is on top of the hill." (That's where the wind turbines were located.) Joni tried to clarify *en français*- Is there an *old* windmill? *Mais oui*, go to the top of the hill, turn right, it is behind some old pine trees. We skeptically drove back up the hill behind the town. Finally, we spotted a few old pines located in the middle of plowed fields. A rutted road took us to, yes, an actual old windmill. No blades left, but still pretty cool. Another adventure checked off the list.

As mentioned in an earlier chapter, sometimes Christian, Juliette and the other workers here at the château humor me by letting me come out and play *vintner* with them. Here is a list of some of the jobs I have done- clean out the grape press, stir all the barrels of wine that are aging, put labels on bottles. I know, not very exciting but I loved every minute of it. I suspect that many of my tasks were things that they really did not want to do themselves. Still fun for me.

One particular day, I was working in the wine vat room where the newest vintage of wine was aging away. One of the guys was up on the vats taking measurements. He called down to me in his slow English (with a French accent), "Can - you - hand - me - a - blewbeek? Eet - eez - on - zee - desk." I went to the desk and frantically searched for something that this could possibly be. The desk, of course, was a mess. Was it a special type of beaker for measuring wine? I saw a blue funnel hanging on the wall. Was that it? "No, no", he says, "the blewbeek?" By this point he's wondering why this daft American can't understand simple English.

After much back and forth that did not clarify anything for me, he climbed down the ladder, grinned at me...and picked up a blue Bic pen from off the desk.

13- Beaujolais and Les Sarmentelles (Chip)

As mentioned in chapter 1, we planned our fall France adventure timeline so that we could attend the world-famous wine celebration called *Les Sarmentelles*. A *sarment* is an extra stem that has been clipped from a vine. This event is held near the end of November, following the end of the grape harvest, when the new vintage of *Beaujolais Nouveau* is released to the world.

A brief explanation is necessary here. The Côte d'Or where we had been living is located in the northern part of Burgundy. Wine there is made using Pinot Noir (red) and Chardonnay (white) grapes. Beaujolais is a wine made in an area just south of Burgundy. They make their red wine using a grape called Gamay. "What's the difference?" you ask. "Isn't all this French wine about the same?" Oh no, no, *non*! According to the people who live in the Cote d'Or, they believe that Beaujolais- both the wine and the area- is inferior to their serious wines and towns. Conversely, the folks who live in the Beaujolais area think the Burgundy folks should get their vines out of their...*derrières*. Of course, I exaggerate, but you get the idea.

Actually, the Beaujolais area makes some very nice wines. They are generally considered to be lighter and fruitier in nature, compared with the drier wines of the Cote d'Or. Nouveau Beaujolais is a wine that they make specifically to be drunk shortly after it is bottled in the fall. Some wine snobs criticize it harshly. One wine critic recently wrote that it was like "drinking fermented grape juice." Another went so far as to say, "Drinking Nouveau Beaujolais is like eating cookie dough." Man, serious joy-stealer! I like to eat cookie dough.

Nouveau Beaujolais is released worldwide on the third Thursday of November. The wine is shipped out earlier but may not be sold or opened until that date. At midnight, corks are pulled all over the world. Many restaurants, bars and wine clubs have release parties on that day. In the days before worldwide distribution, there was a race by some of London's social elite to see who could get the first bottle from Beaujolais, France to their London club. This involved risky automobile drives through France during the dead of night, boat rides across the English Channel and trains to London. Planes were later used when they first came into fashion. From this modest beginning, we now have this mad rush to drink the wine every November. Of course, all this is a very clever marketing tool that the Beaujolais wine makers have embraced to sell a lot of young wine in a very short amount of time.

Joni and I decided to help the French celebrate the release of *Beaujolais Nouveau* wine by attending this festival in the town of Beaujeu, right the heart of the area. Not wanting our Burgundy friends to be offended by what, in their opinion, would be a total waste of time, we snuck out of town and drove south, eagerly anticipating an evening of festivities. The schedule we had seen on the internet looked wonderful but a tad long for us old-timers.

We arrived in the town of Beaujeu a little after noon on a cool day to scope out the situation. The town seemed strangely quiet to us. We parked and found the locations of the various evening events. A few folks were setting up tents and some women were decorating the main street with vine cuttings tied up with ribbons. There were a few cardboard cutouts of men holding wine glasses. All in all, however, the whole scene seemed kind of low key and disappointing. Had we wasted time and money driving down here? We decided that, whatever the evening brought, we were there for an adventure and would enjoy it. Midnight was, after all, a long way off. We headed to our hotel for a late lunch and an afternoon nap.

We drove back to Beaujeu late in the afternoon. We had read horror stories on the Internet about parking being a mess but we found a spot just north of the *centre ville*. The town still seemed to be dead as a doornail. But, as we walked towards the area for the evening's festivities, we heard what seemed to be live music playing on the empty streets. Then someone's voice was talking in a loud, fast and excited manner. We finally realized that, even though we were walking through what could pass as a ghost town, the entire place had been wired for sound with speakers hanging in the trees and on the buildings.

Finally arriving at some wine tasting tents, we saw the source of the music and voices. There were two local celebrities who had been designated as Masters of Ceremony for the event. On their handheld wireless mics, they were dancing to the music and holding roaming interviews. Their mics were being broadcast throughout the village. The music was coming from two guys on golf cart type vehicles. They had converted them into weird Rube Goldberg, one-man-band set ups.

This whole plaza was set up like a county fair. Vendors were getting ready to sell food and goods of all types and kinds. Strolling bands, of the type you might find at Disneyland, were wandering around playing basketball pep band music. Most impressive, however was a tall structure that had been erected near the local church. Several stories tall, it was made of wine barrels on their side stacked up like a pyramid. A couple of hundred people were already milling about. It was nothing like the crowds we were expecting but at least something was going on.

A wine tasting event was underway. For a few Euros, we purchased two commemorative wine glasses and received a contest entry form. We walked around to various tasting stations sampling the different Beaujolais wines. These wines were not Nouveau Beaujolais, but properly aged vintages from the area. The goal was to know or guess the year in which each wine was bottled. This reporter believes it was just an excuse to get the drinking underway early but...whatever! The winner would win their weight in wine. We dutifully tasted all the wines with Joni making her year guesses, often resting her paper on my back in the crowded tents. It was obvious from even the smallish crowd around at that time that this was going to be an internationally attended event, as many languages were being spoken and everyone was of good cheer.

After submitting Joni's tasting guesses, we walked down the road where a huge tent had been erected, much like we had seen earlier in the fall at Oktoberfest in Munich. This was where the *Dîner Spectacle* would be held. It was to feature a multi-course dinner, music by the *Orchestre Tony Bram* and a *Review Exotique*- whatever that was. We were sure the hype would exceed the actual event, but we were only going to come to this once, so adopted a "Let's enjoy it all" attitude. As we entered the tent, we were, of course, some of the first people there. How do the French always know to wait until we have arrived first to all flock in?

We took in an unexpected scene. Although the tent was as big as those we had seen at Oktoberfest, that is where the similarity ends. Inside were hundreds of formally arranged dinner tables. On the tables were name placards, linen tablecloths, two wine glasses each (not plastic), and six pieces of silverware for each person. (My, Toto, we're not at Oktoberfest anymore!) The tables were thoughtfully arranged to give everyone a good view of the large stage set up on one side of the tent. It held enough electronic sound & light equipment to put on a complete Broadway musical.

As we walked in, we were greeted by circus-type entertainers and Miss Beaujolais. A live band was playing. A tuxedoed *maître d'* took us to our table to be seated. As we were shown our seats, a quick calculation showed that there were places for right around 2000 people. We were wondering where all the people were going to come from. No need to worry. Soon busloads of them pulled up and disembarked. As the tent filled up, wine and bottled water were brought to each table. It was all a bit surreal.

After the appetizer had been served, the *Orchestre Tony Bram* took the stage. Calling it an "orchestra" was a stretch. It was a rock band with a couple of brass and saxophone players, some vocalists and a couple of ballroom dancers. Their music had a slight disco-esque flavor to it. However, they played a wide variety of music and were good at what they did. The tenor sax player was really outstanding. He did a version of "Yakety Sax"- not usually one of this reporter's favorite songs- that knocked your socks off.

Throughout the first part of the evening, the MCs would run up onto the stage, making a few announcements or introducing some official or another. At one point they got very excited as they announced the "March of the Chefs." The band played a very formal song while the twenty or so chefs, dressed in long aprons and tall white hats, marched from the kitchen to the stage with great pomp. Later, a member of each nationality represented in the audience carried the flags of their countries on a procession through the crowd.

During another break between songs, a giant fulcrum scale was set up on stage so the winner of the wine tasting contest could receive their weight in wine. The winner himself (That's right; Joni did not win.) was not present. Instead, the MCs had Miss Beaujolais substitute at the weigh in for him. I'm sure she was thrilled for everyone in the audience to find out how many cases of wine it took to lift her up.

The end of this portion of the evening featured various folk songs about Burgundy, Beaujolais, drinking- you get the picture. The MCs announced that, to promote international goodwill, we would all join in the same song. As the music began we all linked elbows and swayed back and forth while *la-la-la-ing* the melody. Joni was looking at me quizzically. She said, "Why are they all singing along to a Shostakovich waltz?" No time to figure that out as another of the roving street bands was wandering through the tent playing more folks tunes.

During all of this, we were being treated to a better meal than you can get at most French restaurants in the USA. A salmon appetizer was served, followed by a lobster and crab bisque that was creamy and delicious. Mind you, this was being served to 1000+ guests all at the same time. An army of servers, directed by headwaiters, was whisking trays of hot food out of the kitchen to tables. The main course was a stuffed chicken breast with cream sauce, zucchini "spaghetti" and a potato concoction. The meal was topped off by a cheese course and dessert. Dee-lish!

Of course, the wine was flowing throughout the meal. Huge troughs, containing many bottles of wine each, were mounted on poles. Four tuxedoed men were carrying these around the tent up on their shoulders. They would stop at each table and drop off more wine, thank you very much.

At some point right before the main course, the stage went black. Next, recorded music started and a spotlight hit a sole male dancer. He was joined on stage by eight female dancers and a *chanteuse*. It looked like we were in for a Vegas-style dance revue- dancers who did a balancing act with their elaborate headwear, and costumes that left little to the imagination. The *Review Exotique* had begun.

Frequent costume changes ensued during this show. At one point the women were dressed like Egyptians and the man like a Pharaoh. Then he was a shirtless cowboy and they were Indian maidens. Between these numbers, the singer came out and led the crowd in tunes like "Life is a Cabaret" or "I Love Rock and Roll" or "Champs Elysées." The *Review Exotique* ended with the singer doing a country-western medley and the troupe doing a country line dance.

While shows like this are not the norm in the United States, they are found in France. Many of you readers may have attended just such a show at the Moulin Rouge or Lido in Paris. We, however, did not expect to see this in a tent in Beaujolais. Just part of the experience.

When the revue had finished, Tony and the band came back on stage. This time they did a lengthy medley of American hits from the 50s to 90s. The singers got to practice their English (e "*Knights een white sa-TEEN*" e).

As the dessert wound down, a final parade through the tent ensued. Led by the MCs, Miss Beaujolais and a marching band, the diners paraded out of the tent. Our watches read 11:30 p.m. Only 30 minutes until *Beaujolais Nouveau* time at midnight!

We had read that a "flaming parade" would go through the town being led by the MCs, and large carts of burning vine cuttings- the *sarments* that gave the festival its name. What we did not realize, however, was that everyone, including us, would be given his or her own flaming *sarment* torch to carry in said parade. It was actually more like a giant version of a sparkler that we used to wave around on the Fourth of July. Was this a good idea for people who had been drinking for several hours? As we exited the tent, we were merged into a massive parade of diners strolling down the streets holding their own flaming torches. It stretched out as far as I could see down the main street of town. What a spectacle. Joni turned to me and said, "It looks a little like we are marching to the castle to capture Frankenstein's monster." As we had been dining in the tent, thousands of people had somehow arrived in town. Streets that had seemed lifeless a few hours earlier were now packed.

Our route brought us back to the town square and the towering pyramid of wine barrels we had seen earlier in the evening. The MCs were gathering the crowd around a stage in front of the barrel pyramid.

Laser light patterns were being shown on the walls of the various buildings and the town church. Tables were set up everywhere with *Beaujolais Nouveau* bottles on them. Music was blaring from everywhere.

A countdown ensued. 3! 2! 1! MIDNIGHT! Fireworks went off. Wine started erupting from the pyramid of barrels flowing down from one to another. Bottles were uncorked everywhere in the plaza and somehow, quite suddenly, thousands of people were all drinking *Beaujolais Nouveau*. Quite a feat on the part of the organizers. The various bands were all playing and people were enjoying the wine. It was not a rowdy crowd but fun-loving and congenial.

1:00 a.m.- Time for the Grand Ball to begin. Dancing to music of- you guessed it- the *Orchestre Tony Bram*. It went until 4:00 a.m. At least that is what we read. We were back in our hotel room, fast asleep by 2:00 a.m. Still, it was a once-in-a-lifetime adventure that we would not have missed for anything.

And that was just our first wine festival of the week.

14- Armistice Day (Joni)

It seems that every town in France, large or small, has an "*Avenue 11 Novembre*" honoring the date when the treaty was signed to end World War I. This is what is called "Armistice Day." The treaty was signed at 11:00 a.m. on the 11th day or the 11th month of 1918.

We attended our village's Armistice Day commemoration. It started with a Mass at the church, where several veterans solemnly marched French flags to the front of the altar and bowed their flags towards the cross.

After the service, everyone went to the town square just outside the church entrance, and waited for the band to line up (the snare drummer was the last to arrive, of course). This band consisted of about twenty townspeople of all ages. The youngest was the little boy whose trombone was bigger than he was. Our friend Juliette was the clarinetist.

The band lined up and marched down to the town war memorial playing marches we had never heard before. As was mentioned in an earlier chapter, there is a war memorial in every French town, naming the soldiers who died in the first and second world wars. Except for the little trombonist, everyone was able to march in step and play at the same time.

At the war memorial, the mayor read the speech that the president of France had read that morning at the Arc de Triomphe in Paris. After a lengthy moment of silence, the band played the national anthem: "*La Marseillaise*."

The whole procession then went back the way they had come, to the town hall courtyard with the band once again playing and leading the way. It was announced by the mayor that everyone was invited into the building to "share a glass of friendship" (that means wine). This was a little after 11:00 am, by the way.

We weren't sure what we should do. Of course, we had already crashed a party in the town hall of Tours after the bike race in October, but we didn't want to go in the town hall here if we shouldn't. Yet, we really wanted to seize the opportunity to go inside this building, which is gorgeous on the outside, and we certainly wanted to participate fully in this event. Finally, I got up the nerve to ask the mayor if it would be alright if we came in, explaining that we were Americans, temporarily living in the village. He replied, "As Americans, of all people you should join us." It was a very touching moment. We went in and were offered glasses of wine, no questions asked. Interestingly, the wine was German. It was made in the sister city to our adopted village. We have noticed that most French towns have German sister cities. These relationships were established after World War II to promote long-lasting peace between the two countries.

There is no school in France on Armistice Day, and the memory of two world wars looms large here. As we drive or hike through small towns, we can't help but think of all of the war movies we've seen, with American GIs carefully entering small French villages searching for and fearing the enemy. As we hike through the woods, we think about the French resistance fighters who may have been hiding in these same woods, or barns, or farmhouses.

One day we were in a small gift shop (imagine that!) and I started visiting with the shopkeeper, who was born in 1927. She talked about the war and about the German planes that had flown over their small town every day. She told me a story about two young men who had hidden weapons inside their Grandfather Clock. The Germans found the weapons; the two were deported and never seen again. She said to make sure to look at their town's war memorial, and that I would see how many people from her town had died in the wars- a large number, she said, for such a small town. She was very proud of the number of Resistance fighters from the village.

She also told me about the German man who moved to her town after World War II. He had flown over the town frequently, because it was on his flight path. He thought it was such a pretty town that, after the war, he bought a house there. It was clear when she told this story that it was a very big deal to have a German move to their town after the war, but she was proud of this, and proud that more Germans moved there after him. She had the wisdom to know that people are people, and that it is important to move on and become friends, even after such horrible events. When I told her that my father had fought in WWII, there were tears in her eyes as she told me how much the French people appreciated the help of the Americans. It was a conversation I will never forget.

15- Les Trois Glorieuses (Chip)

One weekend near the end of our stay we attended another wine celebration that was called *Les Trois Glorieuses-* The Three Glorious Days. A tad more subdued than Beaujolais Days in the south, it was still interesting in its own right. The name refers to a trio of events that occur yearly during the third weekend of November. The first is a dinner and induction ceremony held by the local wine growers' version of King Arthur's "Knights of the Round Table." It is called *La Confrérie des Chevaliers du Tastevin*, or The Brotherhood of the Knights of Wine Tasting. The dinner is always prepared by one of the best chefs in the region. Needless to say, a lot of wonderful wine is poured and consumed. As was mentioned in an earlier chapter, our friend David from Minnesota had been inducted as a member of this prestigious organization. Alas, we could only hear about this event from him because it is not open to the public.

The second event is a formal "black-tie" dinner held at the *Château de Meursault* in the wine town of the same name. This dinner is called *La Paulée,* after a French sauté pan because, when it first began, the meal was so simple it could be made in a single pan. This traditional event is used to celebrate the end of the wine harvest. Each attendee, vintners from the region, brings a bottle of his or her own best wine to share.

The third event is a charity auction held by the *Hospice de Beaune.* More on this auction later.

Since the general public (like us) is either not invited to attend or cannot really afford to partake in these events, the community of Beaune and the surrounding wine villages have decided to have their own festivities, and have turned the long weekend into a public fair of sorts that anyone can attend.

We began our weekend of festivities by going into Beaune on Friday evening to see *Les Lumières*- the lighting up of the town.

As we had strolled around Beaune on our visits in previous weeks, I had noticed work crews putting up row after row of lights above the streets. In just the past week they had also erected some really fancy lighted decorations in the public places and above the entrances to most of the major buildings. Now, during the festival, these would be turned on each night. Our arrival time was perfect. Within minutes of parking our car and strolling to the center of town, on popped all of the various displays. Twinkling lights were everywhere and it made for a magical effect within the pedestrian center of the town.

In addition to the lights, there were tented booths throughout town. These sold local wares such as mulled wine, escargot, *foie gras*, cheeses and other crafts. Our friend, David, had has own booth set up where he was marketing his beautiful stone coasters with imprints of Côte d'Or wine labels.

What I had not realized was that the evening would also incorporate some very high-end projection art shows on a number of the town's major buildings. These shows, which lasted around 5 minutes each, used the building façades as canvases. The creative programming of the projectors lit up the buildings and strategically placed sound systems added music to these shows. We were in awe of how these projections incorporated locations throughout France, snippets of movies or the interiors of the buildings themselves.

We had read that on Saturday the festival was to hold a half-marathon race. We stayed in our village because we had seen on the map that the race was going right through our town, with the halfway point being located in downtown itself. People had told us it would be a "madhouse" but we thought, what the heck, we're here so let's experience it all.

The race began in Beaune at 2:00 p.m. We decided to arrive in the village center at around that time so we could get prime spots to watch the runners. After all, we stood in a packed crowd for almost five hours to see the end of a bike race in Tours! We needn't have worried, however, as the center of town was quite empty, maybe more so than usual for a Saturday afternoon. We went into a local bar for a drink.

Forty-five minutes later, when the first signs of the race were approaching, there was still hardly anyone about- maybe twenty or so of us hardy fans to cheer on the runners. Then the first two runners came through town. They looked like they had not even broken a sweat in the first half of the race. We enthusiastically applauded for them. Due to the scarcity of spectators, as each successive small group as they came by, we felt the need to cheer and clap loudly.

Next larger groups of runners started to trickle through town. These were soon followed by mobs of joggers arriving without breaks. Continuing to applaud each group we felt our hands getting quite tired and sore. We and other spectators were also yelling "Bravo!" and "*Allez!*" (Go!) at all the runners. Some of the runners looked like death. Others were smiling and responding with, "*Merci les spectateurs!*"

There were a wide variety of costumed runners. Some were dressed as wine bottles, corks or corkscrews. Other were striped criminals escaping from the Keystone cops. Runners were from all over the world, including a large contingency from Japan with their "I (heart) Burgundy" t-shirts. I asked Joni, "How many runners do you think there are?" I looked more closely at the entry numbers pinned to their shirts. One high number read 2364. Could that be right? Were there really over two thousand people in this race? Could I applaud for them all? Joni's hands were already looking red.

Hours later, it looked like the final runners had passed us by. We rubbed our tired and swollen hands as we strolled down the road to return to our apartment. Suddenly we saw one lone runner still approaching town. All the official race vehicles were behind her with their lights flashing. We gave her some final feeble applause and words of encouragement. We ran into our friend Juliette and her family. They had been watching the race on the outskirts of town. Juliette told us that this last woman had apparently gotten lost on the route and took a wrong turn. The officials were able to find her and get her turned around. We never did hear if she finished the race, but we hope she persevered.

Sunday saw us up early and back in Beaune. The first event on our schedule was a parade from the church (after Mass) to the town square. It featured a procession of officials from the festival, complete with a statue of St. Vincent, the patron saint of winemakers. Also in the parade were a number of instrumental bands that came to Beaune for the wine festival. Two of these groups really impressed us. One was a band from a canton in Switzerland that was very precise, controlled and musical. The second was a military band from Italy. They were enthusiastic in their marching and playing, almost running down the street. I don't know how they kept their instruments at their mouths to play.

The parade was followed by a ceremony where celebrities who had some connection to Burgundy were inducted into the local wine club. Each year several such figures were invited to attend the festival. They each picked a charity to support with money raised during the weekend. We stayed to listen to a couple of the inductions. One was for a singer and another for an Olympic swimmer. At the wine auction later in the day, a special barrel of wine was auctioned to raise money for one these charities. It was up to the celebrities to "raise the stakes" as high as possible on the barrel so that his or her charity would get the money.

Although there were plenty of normal folks around, on this day we noticed a lot of very well-heeled people in Beaune. Many men were dressed in tailored Armani suits. They were escorting women in gorgeous clothing with Hermès scarves, expensive leather handbags and fur coats. Beautiful Italian shoes and boots adorned their feet. Gold cufflinks and jewelry were everywhere. After thinking and debating this scene for a while, we finally figured out what was going on. These folks with the money were in town for that afternoon's wine auction.

In the early afternoon the wine auction, held by the *Hospice de Beaune*, got underway. The Hospice has been a mainstay in Beaune since the mid-15th century. It was founded by the then-Chancellor of Burgundy as a medical care facility for the poor and needy. Originally located in the *Hôtel-Dieu* it is now a museum honoring the original hospital. The medical facility itself still exists in a newer building nearby.

Throughout the centuries, the Hospice has acquired valuable vine acreage within Burgundy. The first donation of vines took place in 1443, and continues to this day. Much of the land was bequeathed by vintners. Instead of selling this property, Hospice leaders had the foresight to keep the land and hire vintners to look after the grape vines on it. The *Hospice* now owns around 60 hectares of vines in some prime growing spots around the Côte d'Or. (That's about 150 of USA acres.) Some of these plots are designated as *Grand cru* or *Premier Cru* vineyards- the best that Burgundy has to offer.

Every fall after the harvest and pressing of the grapes, the Hospice auctions off its wine juice. Buyers come from all over the world to participate. These buyers, mostly vintners or *négociants* themselves, take delivery of the juice and make it into a special wine that they can sell or keep for their personal cellars. And, once the wine is made, part of the deal is that they can bottle it with a special "Hospice de Beaune" label.

We gathered outside the auction hall with several hundred other people. Large glass windows allowed us to see the tables set up inside for bidders. Many of them were on the telephone to the actual money holders around the world. The auction was broadcast into the public area outside via speakers near the roof. As we listened, each barrel was being sold for about 4,500 to 5,500 Euros. (That is roughly $6000 to $7500 per barrel.) Some went for much more.

Keep in mind that these barrels are only filled with grape juice at this point. The buyers are risking that they can turn this juice into some wonderful wine. We listened as barrel after barrel was purchased, wondering how much money the Hospice was raising. The next day we found out. Joni read in the local newspaper that the auction had raised close to 5,000,000 Euros (almost $7,000,000) for the *Hospice de Beaune*.

We ended our Sunday in Beaune on a much lighter note. One of the local bottling companies was holding a wine-bottle uncorking contest. The goal was to see who could uncork twenty bottles the fastest. Four finalists, all young women, were introduced and brought to the stage with loud cheering. Each ran onto stage to blaring rock/heroic music. They were then interviewed by the MC. Each was asked what kind of corkscrew they wanted to use. The crowd oohed and aahed with each choice. Then it was time for the main event. A countdown started- *trois – deux –un – allez!* As the music blared and the MC screamed about the action, the women pulled corks as fast they could. The first to get her 20 bottles open was greeted by huge cheers from the crowd and Queen's "We are the Champions!" Not sure what she won but she was pretty excited. I hope it was a barrel of *Hospice de Beaune* grape juice.

16. Patience, Please! (Joni)

The first time I did laundry at our apartment, our landlord told me that "In France you have to be patient." When one lives in a foreign country, the many cultural differences do require patience. And one learns that "different" doesn't mean "wrong." Here are some examples of patience on the part of the French and of the two of us.

Doing laundry, as I mentioned above, requires patience for this writer. We had an apartment-sized washing machine that held about half the amount of laundry as does the one I have at home. The first time I did laundry, I wasn't, as Antoine had advised, patient. Since I couldn't believe it could possibly take so long, I started spinning dials around. Everything started all over again, and a small load of laundry sadly took almost six hours to complete.

This machine, which was across the courtyard from our apartment, was my nemesis. When I managed to leave the dials alone during the wash, it took 90 minutes for the load to be done. But wait- there's more. After those 90 minutes, I had to turn the dial to the spin cycle, and it would then spin. Unless, of course, I accidently pressed the button for "no spin," or if I selected "delicate." Then it wouldn't spin no matter what.

One time I just took the dripping wet and unspun clothes out and hung them on the line in the back of the house. It only took another 36 hours for it to dry, and that was with no rain. One day Antoine saw me standing and staring at the machine, so he came in to see what was wrong. Perhaps he had noticed that, for almost three hours, I had been going back and forth into the laundry room. He found me once again messing with the settings. When he asked me what the problem was, I stomped my right foot and said, *"Antoine, je déteste cette machine!"* He carefully reset the dial as I hadn't (apparently) placed it quite right. Then he told me I had to be gentle, like a woman. "Antoine, *I'm* a woman!" He smiled and went on his way.

Chip finally got sick of my complaining and downloaded English-language instructions for the machine. Then it only took two hours to do one small load of laundry.

There was no clothes dryer, so I hung everything out, which is the norm in France. We had a really cool apparatus to use for drying, which folded up and went in the closet when it wasn't in use. You saw them everywhere. By the way, a person has to remember that, when they hang their laundry outside, they have to watch for rain. Otherwise your clothes can hang outside for a really, really long time. I've learned this lesson the hard way. Patience.

While on the topic of laundry, I'd like to add that towels can be very different here. They might be thin and rough, or they might be like sponges that soak up the water but then they remain wet. If I wanted to start a new business in France, I think it would be a towel store with American towels. I could make a mint.

We find the French to be infinitely patient with each other and with us. Lines tend to be long at the nearby supermarket cash register, especially if there is a problem with something when a person is checking out. But people just wait. They don't say a word. Certainly, the person creating the long wait has been, from time to time, yours truly. For example, let's explore the adventure of buying a few apples. At French grocery stores, you weigh all of your own produce and label it, much like you would do in the bulk section in the United States. This took me a very long time, because I had to figure out which code to punch in, and also because I had to get the blasted plastic bags open. They have plastic bags there for their produce that only French people can open, I'm certain. Sometimes I thought there was a hidden camera where the French people could watch the silly American woman wrangle with her "French Only" bag. But I digress.

Back to the apples. I was having difficulty deciding which apple I had on the scale. There were many choices on the screen that accompanied the scale, and the bin of apples had no identifying number with it (usually they do). I took my best guess, based on color and country of origin. When I got to the front of the checkout lane after a long wait, the cashier told me I had picked the wrong apple on the scale. She told me which one to pick and sent me back to reweigh and label my apples. I couldn't find the apple she named as a choice on the scale, so I came back, horrified to see a long line of people waiting at the checkout lane behind my cart. Waiting for me- *l'américaine*. Plus, I had to tell her that I had failed to find the apple she had named on the list of choices. She shook her head with just a bit of disgust, and took my apples to the produce section herself. I followed with my invisible tail hanging between my knees. She went to the scale; she searched for the right apple. She wrinkled up her nose. She flagged down another employee and they discussed this apple situation for a while. She shrugged. Her colleague shrugged. We all came back to the cash register and she typed an amount into the register. The line now extended around a corner. The point here is, besides the fact that they didn't have my apple on their computer system, that not one of those people in line acted impatiently. No one looked at their watch, no words were spoken, there were no dirty looks. Amazing.

By the way, I have found that "country of origin" is very important to Europeans in general. I've been told that the best apples are from Germany, that I shouldn't buy bananas from Cameroon, and that Spain's tomatoes are 'the worst!'

As we have alluded to in other chapters, a person in most towns in France needs to be patient if they want to do any shopping, or any business at all. That is because everything (except for restaurants) shuts down for two hours for lunch, typically from noon until 2:00 pm. Not only that, because businesses are open on Saturdays, they are closed not only on Sundays but also on one weekday. The day varies from town to town. For us, the standard rule of thumb is this: whatever day we arrive in a town, that will be the day where everything is shut down. Patience. The other option, of course, is to find the one restaurant in the area that has chosen to stay open that evening. Not so difficult to be patient when one can have "go out to eat in a French restaurant" as their fall back option.

Lunch is a time-honored tradition in France, which is why the businesses are closed for those two hours. Students come home from school, and most parents come home from work to have lunch together. Work stopped at the vineyard, tools were put down, and everyone paused in their day to enjoy the noontime meal. The typical workday- and school day- goes quite late in the day. The French eat a snack late in the afternoon because, as you'll see below, dinner is eaten later in France.

If you are going to eat out, you'll need to BE patient with that experience as well. As we have written previously, restaurants don't open for dinner until 7:00 or 7:30. When we arrive at 7:30, we are usually the only ones there for another half hour, and people keep showing up until 10:00 for dinner. Because dinner can take a couple of hours or more, restaurants have only one "seating" per night. No one will ever rush you out, and no one will bring your bill until you ask for it. Of course for we Americans, this requires patience. Servers will not be rushing over to take your order. Servers will not be checking in on you every time you take a bite or start a sentence to find out "how is everything tasting so far?" There will be a lengthy pause between courses. In the United States, the philosophy in most restaurants is, get the customer seated, take the order, feed them, and get them out again, so that the next party can use the table. But when you have only one seating per table per evening, that attitude is completely changed. It takes Americans some time to relax and realize that this isn't bad service. It isn't wrong. It is just different. And, I would like to add, *"Vive la difference!"*

When you sit down at a restaurant, there is a plate with an artfully folded napkin on it. Then, when you order, they take the plate away. They will bring you the silverware that you need for your particular entrée. And what the French call an entrée is actually the first course. It could be a salad, ham with parsley, or eggs poached in- you guessed it- wine. The silverware will be brought out on a plate and will be placed rather ceremoniously in front of you. After that course, everything is taken away.

Before the main course, they bring out another plate of silverware and give you what is appropriate for your meal. These are very specific. You will get a different knife depending on whether you order fish, steak or chicken.

After the main course, there might be a cheese course. Sometimes you have the choice between cheese and dessert, sometimes you can order both courses. If you have been drinking white wine with your meal, you would traditionally change to red for the cheese course (although this is slowly changing in this nation of traditions). The course usually consists of one piece of goat cheese, one soft cheese such as a Brie, and one slightly firmer cheese. It can include, however, a bleu cheese, or two soft cheeses, or even more diverse combinations. Sometimes a plate with the three or four cheeses is brought to you to eat from. Sometimes an entire cart of various cheeses is pushed to the side of the table, and you just help yourself to the ones you want. I am happy to be patient if it means that the cheese cart will eventually roll my way.

Before dessert the whole thing happens again, except that this time, they will take a little knife-type thing and will brush all the crumbs from your tablecloth onto a little silver dustpan. I always wonder if I have more crumbs than do the French people. I'm sure I have. This procedure happens at even the smallest country restaurants.

There is no tipping of wait staff. The servers are being servers for their livelihood. It is a career for them. They are paid a living wage and, like all French citizens, they receive health care through their government.

17- Au Revoir (Joni)

Fall was progressing, and the weather in the Côte d'Or was changing. The hillsides in the fall were beautiful with gold and red vine leaves in the vineyards. It also became noticeably cooler. Chip and I both purchased sweaters, and at the grocery store we picked up some instant hot chocolate. The heat was on in the apartment, but we decided we needed to talk to Antoine, our landlord, about turning it up. What is up with this? We two Minnesotans were cold in our sweaters and I would see him running around in short sleeves. Luckily, the apartment had a huge fireplace (you could probably roast a pig in it, and I imagine that over the centuries, people did just that) with which we could temporarily heat up the main floor of our apartment. A certain dog who wasn't supposed to be in our apartment did enjoy his time relaxing by the fire. Don't tell on us.

November. On our last day in our adopted village, the sun came out and the sky turned blue.

We hadn't wanted to sound like anyone should feel sorry for us, so we hadn't been complaining about recent weather. The past two weeks had been mostly clouds, fog and rain. We also didn't think anyone probably wanted to hear that living in an apartment at a French vineyard, even one with hot water heat, could get a little cold and drafty. But on our last day, to have such beautiful weather was like one final gift from God.

After packing and cleaning in the morning, we took one final hike in the glorious weather. We strolled through the hills above our village for over two hours, with only t-shirts, our jackets tied around our waists.

At one point we came out of the woods into a clearing. The view was a vast expanse of vineyards with the hills and trees, still with some fall color, behind them. And one lone vintner pruning his vines. Chip saw the stunned look on my face and the tears welling up. He said, "There's no crying in hiking, Joni!"

This brings me to the topic of things I knew I would miss when we went home.

Anyone who knows me knows that I'm not exactly the outdoorsy type. Yet, one of the things I would miss the most would be the hikes in the hills of Burgundy. Walking in circles at the local mall back in Minnesota was not going to do it for me anymore!

The other big loss for both of us would be the people we'd met, who have become our friends. In previous chapters we have written about some, but not all, of them. These people opened their hearts, and sometimes their homes, to us. If someone ever tells you that the French are distant or rude, don't believe it. Our hearts are full because of the people we came to know and care about.

The kindness our winery family extended to us was more than we could have hoped for. As we have mentioned before, our host, Antoine, had two lovely young adult children: Christian, who worked in the wine business with his dad and who had his own apartment at the property, and Anne, married just over a year (her mom was able to attend the wedding shortly before she passed away) and expecting her first baby in just a few months.

Several other folks, all who have all been mentioned in earlier chapters, became dear to us in our months here. There was Juliette, who worked at the winery and spoke more English than she liked to let on. She worked patiently with Chip when he occasionally helped with some of the winemaking on the property.

In a nearby village lived Bérénice and Arthur, who welcomed us into their home and caves for tastings. She was seventy years old, yet climbing up and down an extension ladder like nobody's business, and was so very proud of their wines and of their lives as winemakers.

The women in the post office are two of the women in my French "sisterhood." When we were at the post office trying to send a package home (yes, we made a few purchases), we couldn't find the packing tape, which I was supposed to have brought. Chip had to go back home to look for the tape, which turned out to be under my seat in the car. Oops. He was none too happy about searching all over the apartment for tape that was already in the car. When I explained this to one of the post office ladies, she said "*merde*" (look it up), and told me I could spend the rest of the afternoon with them if I wanted. Then they wanted to talk about their favorite actors. They were especially interested in George Clooney and Hugh Laurie. Of Hugh, one of them said, "*Nous aimons les 'bad boys'*" (We like the bad boys).

Camille was the woman who worked for one of the local winemakers, spoke English, and did many wine tastings for us and our guests. She was also new to this village but we were certain that she would hit it big when the new local theatre group got up and running, as she had plans to audition. Eva at the tourist office had the patience of Job and answered all of our questions. At the beginning this was a daily ritual. And, we had even made friends with a guy from Minnesota, David. He left his career as an attorney to start his own business (successfully) in Burgundy. I admire his guts; he had been there for eight years. Everybody knew him; everybody liked him, including us.

I could write a book about my friendship with Suzanne. We got together so that I could practice my French and she could practice her English, and became friends for life. She and Samuel, her husband, moved to Burgundy from Belgium after retirement and started making wine. They now sell some of the most expensive wine in the world.

One of my previous chapters was about having patience. Imagine how much patience they had with us! For example, there was the time we were finishing a long hike outside a neighboring town. We were famished but worried that we might be arriving back in the village too late to get any lunch. And I had quite the need for a WC. We didn't know the town at all but found a place with people sitting outside on the patio eating their lunch, and we saw a sign on the door about rooms to rent. So, we hopped up the stairs to the patio, balanced our hiking poles against an outside wall, and started in through the open doorway. Everyone is so friendly here- they all turned and smiled at us. One of the women at the outdoor table said "Bonjour!" and we said "bonjour" right back. Then, she said (in French), "Welcome to our home. This is not a restaurant!" Oops! Unfortunately, in spite of their smiles and the good laugh we all shared, they weren't ready to share their chicken with us. On we went.

Mixed emotions filled us the morning of our departure. We loaded up the car and said our final good-byes. We knew we had succeeded in our goal, but were sadder to leave than we could have ever predicted months ago, when this trip was in the planning stages. The night before, we had been sitting by the fire in our living room drinking some fine wine, the dogs laying in front of the hearth, and we reflected on our experiences. We promised ourselves we would be back soon.

Part Three- Encore

18- The Americans Return...and return...and return (Joni)

By now, you should know that we had no regrets taking three months out of our lives to live like locals, or at least try to, in a foreign country. Something that we didn't anticipate was that we fell more in love with Burgundy than we could have imagined. We love our own home in Minnesota, our friends and of course our family. But there was something about the French culture that pulled at our heartstrings, and we knew we wanted to go back.

We are fortunate. We have found the means to go back to France several times. Had it not been for Covid-19, as a matter of fact, 2020 would have been our sixth long-term stay in Burgundy. We know that with so much loss associated with that pandemic, our loss of a fall in France is a small thing.

This section of the book contains stories from several of our later stays in France. No matter how many times we have the good fortune to return, we know one thing for sure: there is always more to learn for these two American Francophiles. We'll get started by sharing with you our adventures when we returned to France the following fall.

The day of our departure from Minnesota was quite relaxing. We took a late afternoon flight to Chicago for a transfer to the Paris flight. Upon arrival at the airport, check-in was a snap, with no one else in line at the counter. The security lines were as short and as fast as we had seen them in a quite a while. We got to our gate in plenty of time, much more relaxed than we had been one year earlier.

We did have a concern about our connecting flight in Chicago, as we only had one hour to change planes. As it turned out it was not a problem because the Chicago-Paris flight was boarding late. There had been a problem with the plane's cooling system, and it was too hot to get on. Chip saw the crew coming off before we were told this and said, "They look like they were just in a sauna." After a thirty-minute wait while they "cooled the plane down," we boarded a very warm plane.

We then went through the usual routine of trying to ram everyone's carryon bags in the space above the seats. After that drama, we sat for about ten minutes. The crew then came on the PA and told us we would need to deplane because of an electrical problem they could not fix. So...out came all the carryon luggage and off we all went.

Unfortunately, at least half of the plane's passengers were French, and nothing was said to them in their native language even though there was a French-speaking flight attendant on board. The woman behind us, for one, was very confused and I did my best to help her understand. Those of us who spoke French and English tried to keep the French-only speakers informed. I felt bad for them. The Frenchwoman behind us kept saying that this "would never happen on Air France." "We would have wonderful cookies waiting for us." "These people are so impolite!" She was right about that one. But I'm guessing French planes have mechanical problems once in a while, too. ;-)

During the delay, we were given soda, water and little bags of trail mix in the gate area. When they finally realized they were going to have to get a different plane for us and the delay would be more than an hour, they handed out $12 vouchers for dinner as well. We went to get dinner with $12 burning a hole in our pockets. That amount of money at O'Hare airport does not go very far. As a matter of fact, it barely paid for our beverages. Nevertheless, we picked up some fast food and made our way back to the gate.

While we waited at the gate, I struck up a conversation with an American woman whose son was a journalist for a cycling magazine. We started talking about the Tour de France. I told her I was a big fan of the tour and Lance Armstrong. She confidently told me that, "everyone knows Lance Armstrong was doping." I boldly defended him. She rolled her eyes at me as if I were the most naïve person on earth. I got a little huffy. It was less than four months later that the world learned that Armstrong *had* been doping...and he admitted it. I have since also realized that I should not invest money with Bernie Madoff, Richard Nixon *was* a crook, and not everything I read on the internet is 100% true.

Our flight ended up being delayed four and a half hours. After boarding and take off, they immediately served dinner again. Which was better...airport fast food or airplane food? That's a toss-up. The poor Frenchwoman seated behind me was dissatisfied with both!

We arrived in France, went through passport control, got our baggage, and called for our lease car. Our driver fetched us and took us to the car park to pick up our car. On the way, he wanted to teach me French swear words. I told him that I had once mistakenly said the "F Word," when I meant to say "kiss". Oops. He said in perfect English, "Oh, yeah, that word means F—-". Just as blasé as could be. After filling out lots of papers, we got in our brand-new Peugeot 308 and set off. So far; so good...

...until we got to the gas station near the airport to fill our near-empty gas tank. Half of the pumps weren't functioning, and the lines were long. After our third try, Chip finally pulled up in front of a pump that seemed to be working. Nothing like maneuvering a brand-new car that we aren't used to around a very crowded gas station area with a bunch of frustrated drivers in it. As per their instructions on the pumps, I went inside to pre-pay, but, as I was telling the attendant we were at Pump 9, another attendant came out and told Chip he had to move from that space. Then, two motorcycles pulled into that pump and started pumping gas with no problem. Fortunately, I got my card back before she ran through *their* charge.

Frustration. Off we went down the freeway on fumes to another gas station; problem solved. But this time we also ran into a delay. Just as we were pulling out of the station and back onto the freeway, we were stopped by officers in uniform. In Europe, gas stations are immediately off the highway, much like how our rest areas are set up in the United States. They were waiting right before the acceleration ramp back onto the autoroute.

One of them approached our car and introduced himself. It turned out that they were customs officers looking for illegal contraband. Although he had a lot of questions, he was so friendly that it seemed like he was more of a one-man welcoming committee for his country than a highly trained government enforcer. Ah, those snobby French you always hear about!

I'm not sure how Chip stayed alert enough to get us to Burgundy and our village, but he did. No thanks to me, who slept much of the way.

We arrived at our familiar apartment late in the afternoon, feeling the effects of a very long travel day from Minnesota. There to greet us was Christian, along with the two dogs. It felt so good to walk into "our" apartment and feel familiar with everything. Finally, a calm spread over us.

Later that day we met the newest member of Antoine's family: Anne stopped over so that we could meet her eight-month old son, Etienne. He was completely fine letting his American Aunt Joni hold him.

We walked into the town center to get a light supper, but of course couldn't resist a three-course meal. And some wonderful Burgundian wine. We sat outside at a table and ate as night fell and the lights came on to illuminate the buildings, just like out of a movie. The church bells reminded us of the time every fifteen minutes. We strolled- or perhaps the word "stumbled" would be more accurate- back to our apartment. The sleepy streets were silent, and even the neighborhood dogs were quiet as we passed their gates. Exhausted but happy, we climbed the stairs to our lovely apartment, and knew we were once again "at home."

The following day we headed into a larger neighboring town for groceries. We ran into Eva, the woman who worked in the village's tourist office during our previous stay. She had told us she was pregnant last fall and now here she was with her four-month old son. We had just been saying how glad she would be to be home with her baby this fall instead of having to help us so much with all of our questions. With all of the tourists who pass through this area, what does it say about us that she immediately recognized us in the grocery store one year later? Don't answer that.

While in this larger town, we also stopped in at a travel agency to book train transportation and two nights in London. Sound crazy? We have one son, Joe, who is an actor/singer/pianist/composer. He had recently been the lead actor, as well as composer and lyricist, for an independent movie musical. Well, while we were flying and driving to our destination in France, it had been announced that the film was selected to be shown at a film festival in London in a few weeks. It seemed a little silly to book a trip to a foreign country on our first full day in another foreign land, but we are always ready for just one more adventure!

19- Harvesting Wine Grapes (Joni)

The fall grape harvest, or *la vendange,* was to begin in about ten days.

I have mentioned my friend, Suzanne from time to time. Suzanne and Samuel, her husband, moved to the village from Belgium. A retired photographer, he had always wanted to try his hand at making wine. He bought some rows of grapes. Not satisfied with doing things the usual way, he decided to employ some non-traditional methods to his wine making. Just to name a couple of these, he used horses to plow the weeds between his rows of vines, removed excess foliage on the vines by hand, and stomped his own grapes. Soon his wine had developed quite a reputation and he was selling his quite small quantity of bottles per year for a very hefty price.

This year, Samuel wanted to make a sparkling wine for the first time. To make a sparkling wine, vintners eventually must add sugar to a white wine. For this reason, Samuel wanted to harvest some of his grapes early before they became too sweet.

We were invited to help with their harvest, if even for just a few hours. We ended up spending most of the day working amongst the vines, and it was a wonderful adventure.

We started out by meeting at their home in town at 8:00 a.m. There were eight people in our merry band. The other workers (all much younger than ourselves) came from a variety of places and backgrounds. There was one couple from a nearby town, one man from Paris and another from Belgium. There was a young lady named Sarah who, along with Samuel himself, was really in charge of our work. Also with us was a young man, Andrew, from the British island of Jersey, who was doing PhD work at Oxford. This geography student was writing his doctoral thesis on the topic of *terroirs,* a French word that has no English translation. The *terroir* is a combination of soil, climate and vegetation that work together to produce the wine that is particular to an area. Smart man. With this research as a great excuse, our new friend Andrew had a perfectly justifiable reason to spend weeks in France visiting different wine regions, interviewing various wine makers, and (of course!) sampling the products.

We drove about five miles to a small plot of Samuel's Chardonnay vines outside a neighboring town. Even at that early hour, the sun was beating down on the warmest day we had ever experienced in Burgundy. We were each given a bucket and a clipper. We were briefly instructed as to how to go about harvesting the grapes. It involved leaning, bending and/or kneeling, clipping the grape bunches from the vines, removing the dead grapes from the bunch and trying not to cut oneself with the clippers. You then put the bunch of grapes into your bucket and periodically emptied your bucket into a larger container. This morning's task was to harvest from eight rows of vines that were about as long as a football field.

After about an hour of work we all took a break for coffee (which they had brought along in carafes) and snacks. Then we were back at it again for about another hour to finish off these rows. Next, we hopped back into our cars and drove to just outside of our village, where we began harvesting in a field of Aligoté vines. Aligoté is the primary grape that Burgundians use for making their sparkling wine. We worked another hour or so, then had our next break. No coffee this time; instead we drank some of Samuel's wine. Fortified yet again, we worked for another 45 minutes or so. Lunch break was declared and we all drove to Samuel and Suzanne's home in the village for our noontime meal.

Suzanne, who is a wonderful cook, had prepared a beautiful meal for us, but first we were each given a glass of sparkling wine. They have a lovely little courtyard where we sat at two outdoor tables, encircled by Suzanne's vegetable garden, which wraps along the whitewashed walls of the space. A stairway led up one level to her dining room, where we helped ourselves to a buffet of vegetarian salads, spinach pizza, bread and cheese. Of course, wine was served with the meal. Finally came a dessert of rice pudding topped with apricot sauce, along with coffee. At this point, it really felt like naptime to the two of us, but instead we bravely went back to the vineyard where we worked another 90 minutes or so. We were finished before 4:00 p.m.

When we got home after all of this, we were sore all over from the bending our bodies had endured and we were totally exhausted. For the first time, we took advantage of the swimming pool in the back of "our" property, and cooled ourselves down. It was great.

The following morning, Suzanne came over and brought us a little bottle of the grape juice from the grapes we had harvested the day before. Samuel thought we might be interested in sampling the juice. Suzanne explained that after we left, Samuel had put the grapes into his electronic grape press (not to be confused with the older one he sometimes used to actually stomp the grapes himself, *à la* "I Love Lucy").

The press gently squeezed the juice from the grapes. Next, this juice went into a barrel where it would age for one year before being bottled.

It would then be stored for another three years before it was ready to be drunk. Just like everything else in France- the time it takes to get the meal you ordered; the time it takes for the shopkeeper to answer all of the questions imaginable to the person in line in front of you (no matter how many people are waiting in said line); the nearly-two-hour cycle of a French washing machine- there is no rush and there is no point in becoming impatient. Especially in the case of French wine and food. Good things come to those who wait!

We walked over to Suzanne and Samuel's later that afternoon, where he showed us his barrels of wine, including the one that was filled with the juice from the grapes we helped to harvest. We drank wine that had been made from grapes of the neighboring plot of land from where we had been harvesting the previous morning. A pleasant hour of relaxing with friends passed quickly. Samuel sent us home with a bottle of wine from his own vineyard. We didn't expect any gift for participating in what we considered a great harvest experience, but we happily accepted his generosity just the same.

Elsewhere in the village, we could feel the anticipation of the true harvest period due to the sudden flurry of activity. It was to begin in about a week's time. Everywhere we walked we saw tractors, trailers, barrels and vats being prepared. Equipment was being set up and cleaned in the vintner's courtyards. Daily, people were driving out into the fields to check the status of their grapes.

Christian told us there would be 25 grape pickers staying at his *domaine* beginning the following Monday. To accommodate them all, there were two large dormitory-style apartments on the property, one being right next to our apartment. We had always wondered what was behind that door! Some vintners have begun using mechanical grape harvesters in lieu of human pickers. This is not as popular in Burgundy as in other parts of France. Here at Christian's property, thirty per cent of their grapes were to be picked mechanically; all the rest would be done by hand. Having now experienced first-hand with Samuel how many people and how many person-hours it takes to harvest a very small amount of grapes, we looked around us at the unending fields and rows of vines and wondered how on earth it all would get done.

20- La Vendange- The Main Harvest Event (Chip)

La vendange (the grape harvest) was in full swing in Burgundy. When the grapes reached the proper sugar content to produce the wine they wanted, it was important for them to be harvested as quickly as possible. Our small adopted village now had many more people around who were here just to work the harvest. Between them and the steady flow of tourists who had come to see the harvest, cars were parked in every nook and cranny. Tractors and trucks pulling wagonloads of grapes traveled through town at all hours. Stores and restaurants altered their hours. And I was able to view it all from the countryside while on my hikes and simply by looking out the window of our apartment into the courtyard.

Here at "our" winery, the extra workers had arrived and moved into the various apartments. Some of them looked like hippie wannabes who were working the harvest as a lark. Others had a loose connection to someone who was a friend of the family. Some looked like serious pickers who traveled south to north throughout France with the grape harvests. A few were local friends of the family who had worked their harvest for years and just enjoyed having a hand in this most traditional of French customs. It was quite the eclectic collection. There were guitars and drums being played during breaks, juggling antics, as well as games of *pétanque* (bocce ball) in the courtyard before dinner. They would harvest most of Antoine's grapes that were planted on 8 *hectares* (just under 20 US acres), and would work here for about a week.

Of course, when something exciting was happening, I would go out to the wine making facilities on the property to have an up-close look without (hopefully) getting in the way. I kept reminding myself that this winemaking business is not just a lark for these people but their livelihood, and, especially at this time, they were all *very* busy.

During the harvest, the first tractor rumbled through town early in the morning, just before 6:30 a.m. Pulling its empty wagon, it bumped loudly down the street. I know because it woke me up. One of our friends, who recently visited to area, observed as we were driving around the countryside that there were no farmhouses or barns out amongst the fields. True. The French farmers mostly live in the villages with everyone else. Their versions of barns are outbuildings connected to or near their houses in town. So, all the tractors and trucks made the daily drive out into the vines.

The first machinery here at the winery came to life a little before 7:00 a.m. It was a grumpy old diesel tractor that sounded like it didn't want to be awake any more than I did. The starter cranked over for maybe 20 seconds- rann, rann, rann, rann, rann, rann... Then the engine coughed and sputtered to life. The engine was revved to keep it going- runnn, runnnnn, runnnnnnnnnn...pfht, pfht, pfht (Will it stay running this time?) pfht...pfht......pfht........pfht............ (Nope.) It sounded like my first old Chevy that had carburetor problems. After several rounds of this, the engine finally held and off they went. As an aside here, for those of you who love machinery like I do, especially things you can drive around, they had lots of nifty pieces of gear around the property. I really wanted to go out and ask Christian if I could just drive around in each powered vehicle for 10 minutes or so, but I had the good sense not to.

The harvesters' day started early. Departure for the fields was before the sun was up. These hearty folks would then pick grapes until around noon, with a short mid-morning break. After a short lunch in the fields, it was back to work until at least mid-afternoon.

As they worked, each picker deposited their grape bunches in small buckets that they carried with them. Other workers walked up and down the rows with large baskets *(vendangeoirs)* strapped to their backs. The smaller buckets were emptied into these *vendangeoirs*. Once their large baskets were full, these folks walked to the end of the rows where a large wagon was parked. They climbed up the side and bent over to empty their basket into the wagon. They then chalked a mark on the wagon to indicate the count of filled *vendangeoirs* in it. Then it was back up the rows to the pickers where the whole process started over again.

As wagons were filled they were driven back to the winery, where the grapes were unloaded. Here the vintners and their assistants took over. The Pinot Noir grapes, for red wine, went through a de-stemming process using a special machine that separated grapes from the stems. They were then deposited in large vats to start the vinification process that used yeasts to convert the grapes' sugars into alcohol.

The Chardonnay grapes, for white wine, were treated differently. They were put into a large rotating press. As an inflatable bladder within the press expanded outward the Chardonnay juice came out and was pumped into vats of its own. The reason these grapes were done in this fashion was to keep their grape skins from affecting the wine's final color. If a wagon of grapes could not be processed right away, dry ice was added to it to keep the grapes cool.

My alarm went off at 6:15 a.m. I know that does not sound early to some of you, but these days, for retired-me, it was. I was excited, however, because I had been invited to work with the harvesters that morning.

After a hasty cup of coffee and some breakfast, I gathered in the courtyard with the other harvesters in the dark. Breakfast for the workers was always coffee, juice, yogurt, and bread...the usual French breakfast staples. I made trouble with the two dogs, while the workers drank coffee and (some) smoked.

Christian took one look at me, turned around, and went back into his apartment. He came back out and gave me a pair of rubber boots to wear in lieu of my white, American athletic shoes. These boots were similar to what my sister-in-law wears around her horse barn. I was soon to find out why. Eventually the harvest leader rang the bell hanging by the large kitchen. That was the signal to load up in various vehicles to drive out into the vines. As we rode along, I looked out over the valley and up the side of the hill with all the vines. Dozens of tractors with their rotating orange lights on top were traveling here and there out to their own plots to harvest.

We began by picking grapes in about ten rows of Chardonnay just south of town. As we walked into the rows and started to cut bunches of grapes, I realized why Christian had given me the boots. The soil between rows had turned to a sticky, clay-like material because of rain the previous day. Within minutes I was clomping around with about five pounds of this goop stuck to each boot. No one else seemed to be having trouble staying upright while walking. Onward.

After a few rows of vines, I could tell that my back, in its current arthritic and aged condition, would be really hurting when we were done. I was constantly kneeling down or bending over the vines to search out each bunch of ripe grapes. Each time I uncurled myself to move to the next vine, I seem to be farther behind the folks in the surrounding rows. When I reached the end of my assigned row everyone else was already headed back down their row double-checking for missed bunches.

When we got back to where we started, everyone was trying to get the muddy goop off their boots. Some were scraping with their cutters and others were trying to slide it off in the gravel road. Some were using the wire strung to hold up the vines to scrape it off. It was a pretty comical sight especially given that a number of them were trying to smoke a quick cigarette at the same time. Now I knew why the seats in our vehicles were covered with black plastic and why cardboard was on the floors.

We next drove to the *clos* (walled area) directly behind our apartment. My back was screaming at me, "PLEASE, go into your apartment and get me some Advil!" I didn't. We harvested from many rows there.

Next it was off to some fields near a neighboring village. This time it was Pinot Noir grapes. The ground was less sticky here, but the terrain was much steeper. Of course, I did not want to lose face by telling anyone how stiff I was getting or how much my back hurt. Christian, however, came to my rescue. "*Cheep* (That's his version of Chip), after these rows come with me in the truck to make a delivery." I said, "OK, if I can be of some help." (My back muscles, however, were doing a little jig of joy.) By this time, we had been doing this for four hours. I know I'm not as young as I used to be but, I have to say, I could not imagine how these people did this for a week (or more!) straight, let alone a full day. Hats off to them!

During the vendange, evening meals were taken in a communal fashion. Antoine's daughter, Anne, was in charge of the kitchen and cooking during the harvest. All of the meals were prepared here at the property for the workers; no ordering in of fast food or take-out pizza. Joni, Madeleine (Christian's girlfriend) and Adèle, a family friend, had been in the kitchen helping out. Joni seemed to fit in well. During the day, various people dropped into the kitchen to say *"Bonjour."* They all gave each other the cheek-to-cheek kisses, called *la bise*, which is the traditional way the French greet each other. Even Joni was included and she was thrilled to feel so French.

We were invited to eat dinner with the family and workers on two nights. After the bell in the courtyard rang announcing dinner, around thirty people sat down together. To signal the beginning of the meal, someone shouted "*Bon Appetite!*" and everyone yelled "*Merci!*" On the night after I had helped with the harvest we had a green salad and a wonderful dish of mashed potatoes with seasoned ground beef and pork. Joni had expertly peeled the potatoes earlier in the day. Bread, wine, beer and water were, of course, present as well. Dessert was homemade applesauce with ice cream. Yummy! Again, Joni excelled at apple peeling.

As we ate, Anne's baby, Etienne, played in a makeshift playpen made out of a grape-harvesting container. The two dogs cleaned up under the tables and helped entertain Etienne. The wine and beer flowed at dinner; the conversation, subdued at first, got progressively louder. Tonight, Joni was trying to teach Anne to say the English word "burp." She went to her brother, Christian, and said in English, "You burp." Christian, however, thought she had said that he had "boobs."

Apparently, something was lost in the translation. At the end of the meal, some of the harvesters cleaned up the kitchen while others socialized and smoked in the courtyard.

As each vineyard finished its harvest for the season, they had little traditions that were carried out. Some of these were as simple as gathering all the pickers in amongst the vines to share some bottles of wine. Others took their trucks and tractors on a honking tour through the villages announcing that they were done.

At our place, Christian, who had a fun sense of humor, had a slightly more elaborate tradition. We arose on the last morning of the harvest to find the plane tree in the courtyard decorated like a Christmas tree, only with ladies' undergarments. Bras and panties of all colors were flapping in the breeze. And, to top it off, there was Christian dressed in white nurse's stockings up to mid-thigh. Above these he wore the shortest shorts I had ever seen, a bra on over the top of his skin-tight shirt, and gaudy make-up on his face complete with lipstick.

Word on the streets of the village was that the year's grape harvest appeared to be smaller than normal. In fact, Joni later read that, overall, the French grape harvest had been determined to be the smallest in two decades. Here in the *Côte d'Or,* there had been two hailstorms earlier in the summer that damaged the vines and grapes. They also had lots of rain and not enough heat. We heard from Antoine that the plot of grapes the family usually harvests for their premier white wine was so badly damaged that it would not even be picked this year. Daughter Anne told us, "The birds will eat them all and get drunk." Both Antoine and Christian took it all in stride. I suppose they are well aware of the ebb-and-flow of harvests over the years and decades. Besides, if the wine is better than average and there is a smaller amount made...they can hopefully charge more when it matures.

21- London and The Chunnel (Joni)

When we made arrangements to come to France for our second fall, we decided to once again stay in our village and our now-familiar apartment. The previous fall we made overnight side trips to Munich, Beaujolais and the Loire Valley. Although these side trips were fun, it seemed silly to be paying for hotel rooms as well as an apartment. This time around, we were going to simply take some day trips within the Burgundy region and leave the larger explorations for the end of our visit.

That was before our son Joe starred in an independent musical movie, which became a selection for the Raindance Film Festival in London. Joe was the lead actor in the movie, but also composed the music and wrote the lyrics for the songs in the film. In fact, after the director met with Joe and hired him, he changed the name of the main character in the movie to Joe's name. So, somewhat surreally, he was playing a character of an up-and-coming music composer as he actually was in real life. And the movie title had his name in it: "How Do You Write a Joe Schermann Song".

After post-production work, the film was sent out to various film festivals in the hopes that two or three might decide to include it. The film was screened at several festivals throughout the United States, with very positive reviews, and won quite a few festival awards. If we had been home in Minnesota we could have seen the film at a nearby festival in Wisconsin. Instead it was off to London to see our son on the big screen.

We hated to leave because it was the last day of the harvest at the winery. We no doubt missed quite a celebration.

We drove as far as Fontainebleau, which is about thirty minutes from the outskirts of Paris. We have found that this is a fantastic way to get into Paris without the hazards of driving into that busy city. You can park (and pay) at the Fontainebleau train station and take the commuter train into the city. We stayed at an "Ibis Budget" hotel. On their website, it said that it was a "cocoon-style" hotel. We had no idea what that meant. Now we know. Truthfully, it was very clean and the staff was very helpful. However, this was a bare-bones room. In fact, in addition to the bed (with a four-inch-thick mattress), the only piece of furniture was a plastic square box, which was our chair. There were no pictures on the walls; there was no ornamentation of any kind. It felt exactly like we had checked into a college dorm room, except that there were no parties down the hall.

The next morning it took some maneuvering to get to where the Eurostar train departed for London. We walked to the Fontainebleau train station and took the forty-minute commuter train into Paris. From that station, we took the *métro* (subway) to another train station, and there we found the Eurostar train. This is the very fast train that runs from Paris to London in two and a half hours by way of the Chunnel. When you consider that it takes an hour to cross the English Channel by ferry, and that it takes our Minnesota Ambassadors student group an entire day to get from London to Paris, this is truly an efficient way to travel.

We had our luggage and ourselves examined by x-ray, much like airport security except that we could keep our shoes on. We boarded thirty minutes prior to "take off" and found our reserved seats in a clean, comfortable car.

We watched as the train got up to speed during the first twenty minutes or so of the journey. Soon we noticed that we were passing cars on the autoroute like they were standing still. We later read that the train goes up to 300 kph (185 mph).

Going through the Chunnel itself was quite anti-climactic. You could easily sleep through it (which I did on the way back to Paris). There is no stopping or even slowing down, and you don't notice that you are headed deep beneath the ground/water. It just looks dark outside of your window, exactly as if you were on a subway. We were in the Chunnel for about twenty minutes, and then, before we knew it, we had reached London.

Our hotel was part of a package deal that we got with our train tickets. It was a huge hotel that catered to groups. Well, I'll rephrase that. This hotel did not actually *cater* to anyone. They *housed* groups.

Before I say more about the hotel let me say that I love London and have found that Londoners are some of the friendliest and most helpful people I've ever met. You can be standing on a street corner looking confused, and a Londoner will come over to you to see if there is any way they can help you.

Not at this hotel. Three men stood behind the concierge desk and scowled at you if you looked like you might approach them. Need a map of London? That would cost two pounds. Need to know where breakfast is? Don't bother looking for a sign or an arrow. Ask the frowning woman at the reception desk and she'll roll her eyes at you while pointing around the corner. When you get to breakfast, you find yourself in a room that feels very much like a lunchroom at a junior high except that no one is throwing food. The men working there did all they could to make you want to leave quickly while they barked orders at the customers: "Sit there!" "No, not there!" "You need to move over!" "You can't save seats!" The lack of respect from the employees led to a lack of respect from the customers, who became (justifiably) angry and were rude back to the employees. It all made me want to budge in line and ask for a pass to the bathroom.

Need the free WiFi that was promised? Only works in the lobby. There was a shoebox on the concierge's counter, and there were many slips of paper in the box with passwords on them. Grab a slip of paper, find a spot in the lobby that isn't already occupied by one of the many people doing the same thing that you are, log in and wait. It might work.

Well, you get what you pay for. It was a good location, and the room was clean and had a chair that wasn't a plastic box. We spent two nights in London, and since we are both retired teachers, we had little problem dealing with the disrespect, although I would have loved to have called the employees' parents for a little chat!

Since the film screening wasn't until the evening of our second day there, we were able to do some sightseeing in London. We went to the British Library, where we saw documents ranging from Leonardo da Vinci sketches to the first compilation of the books of the New

Testament. We saw the hand-scrawled lyrics of "Yesterday" (Paul McCartney) and "Help!" (John Lennon). There were original scores of Mozart's Horn Concerto Number 3, Beethoven's Pastoral Symphony, Mendelssohn's "Wedding March" and Grainger's "Country Gardens". The hand-written manuscripts of these four composers were so sloppy I don't know how anybody ever deciphered them, but somehow these gentlemen managed to make a name for themselves in spite of this. Also on view was the Magna Carta, one of the most famous documents in the world.

We finished off our first evening with a "Harry Potter" walking tour. It took us to some lovely areas, some still lit by gaslight, not electricity. The tour included a stop at Australia House, (a.k.a. Gringotts Bank to you Harry Potter fans), and ended at King's Cross Station, platform 9 ¾. Our tour guide, dressed in his Gryffindor hoodie and scarf, was dramatic and entertaining.

The next day brought more sights and tours in London. When in London with the Minnesota Ambassadors, we always drive past Westminster Abbey, but never have time to go in. Chip and I took a ninety-minute guided tour of this beautiful building, seeing the resting places of kings, queens, and others – including George Frederick Handel, who has a huge monument dedicated to him, in spite of his being German.

We went on a guided tour of the Wimbledon Tennis Club. We hopped on the "tube" and rode out to the end of the line, to the village of Wimbledon. It is now a posh suburb of London. Although it was a very pretty place there was no tennis center in sight. We asked a man selling produce how to get there and he told us we needed to take a bus. So, we went to the bus stop where a fellow passenger helped us get on the right bus and told us when to get off and where to walk from there. Obviously, she and the produce man were not employed by our hotel. They were way too helpful.

The tour of the famous Wimbledon Tennis Club was really well done. We learned that the actual Wimbledon Tennis Club has less than 400 members, and their dues are less than $100/year. Most of the club's nineteen grass courts are only used for the two weeks of the championships. Members don't ever get to play on them, although there are another 36 other courts they can use. The proceeds from hosting the Wimbledon Championship are enough to pay for these beautiful facilities on about forty acres of land.

We also visited the Churchill War Rooms used in World War II. These are located in an underground bunker not far from Buckingham Palace. The maps, the meeting rooms, the beds, the switchboards and the stories recorded on videotape from those who worked there all created a chilling image of what it must have been like to have lived in London during the war. If you go to London, I highly recommend visiting these rooms.

The main event of our trip took place that evening. We took the underground to Piccadilly Circus. I naïvely thought we'd just easily spot the "Apollo Theater Piccadilly Circus" when we got there. What was I thinking? We asked someone; they gave us directions. In the pouring rain, we arrived at the Apollo Theater, but it was a theater for plays, not movies. Fortunately, an employee there got us headed in the right direction, and we eventually found the Apollo CINEMA Piccadilly Circus. My husband didn't scold me for not bringing the address (much), and we had a nice Italian meal before the screening.

As we arrived back at the theater from dinner, we were able to meet the filmmaker/director, Gary, and his wife, as well as one of Joe's co-stars, Christina.

Watching a movie with your son in the starring role is quite an experience, especially since he did a great job. Well, the part where he is embracing a woman in her underthings was a little creepy, but I guess it could have been worse. I already knew that his music was top-notch, but to hear it, to hear him singing and to hear an orchestra backing him up was a wonderful experience. So glad I paid for those piano lessons. "Bloody brilliant!" "Disgustingly talented!" In a British accent these comments sounded even better! It was fun hearing strangers say things about Joe that his family has known all along. It was also fun to hear women in the theater bathroom singing his music and discussing the film after the screening ("How *do* you write a Joe Schermann song? They bloody didn't answer that question in the movie, did they now?").

[Chip here. I just have to insert into Joni's description that she was quite excited and jittery about seeing this movie at the festival. Beforehand, she could not stop grinning from ear to ear. When the lights went down, the music started and Joe's name came up on the screen, I thought she was going to break my left arm, she was squeezing it so hard. I'm not sure how many Kleenex she went through. After the movie, there was a question-and-answer session about the film. I had to hold her arm down from putting up her hand, not to ask a question, but to offer up additional information about Joe to the audience. All in all, it was quite cute.]

Our village was much quieter than it had been before we left for London. Nearly all of the grapes had been picked. Although the hectic pace of the harvest was fun, it was nice to have things back to normal. A hike for Chip, a bike ride for me, leftover Beef Burgundy for dinner. Just another day in France.

22- Old Things (Chip)

It was a lovely late-fall day. When I think about how the Côte d'Or (Golden Slope) was named I believe it must be because of this time of the year. The vines on the hills had turned to beautiful shades of gold and deep red. The bright sun and deep blue sky made the whole scene magical.

Solitary walking gives one a lot of time to think about things. For example, as I walked in the vineyards past vines I began thinking about how old they were. From an earlier conversation with Christian I had learned that the older vines in this area had been producing grapes for 60 years or more. In other words, they may have been planted the year I was born. In the Midwest of the USA, a crop only lasts one growing season, and the average apple tree lives only about 30 years. These vines were old and gnarled. Do I look like that? I don't feel as old as they look. To make me feel better, let me tell you about some things we have seen in France that are way older than all of us.

During our stays in this area, we have visited several castles and *châteaux*. Nearby is the *Château de Sully*. As with many of these French *châteaux* it was originally built in the Middle Ages as a fortified castle complete with moat, drawbridge, etc. During the Renaissance Period, when peace more frequently ruled the land, they were often remodeled into what amounted to luxury estates for the wealthy who desired to escape the squalor of Paris.

I have written about Sully for two reasons. One, it is a great example of how many really old buildings are still standing in this country and throughout Europe. It is not at all unusual to find plaques on walls that report the age of the building to be from the 13th, 14th or 15th centuries. Some are older than that. This thought made me feel positively young! The second reason is that I had read an interesting story about Sully that I thought was worth sharing. I freely admit it has little to do with the topic of age, but it's a good tale nonetheless.

In the 18th century, *Château de Sully* was owned by several brothers. Finding life a tad dull in the country, one of the brothers decided to liven things up by marrying his 19-year-old cousin. It should be noted that he was over 60 years of age at the time. His young cousin, Charlotte, did liven things up for him...perhaps a little too much. A Scottish doctor was called in to see to his health. When the old guy kicked the bucket, the young and widowed Charlotte ended up marrying the Scottish doctor! Since that time, the *Château de Sully* has been owned by the Scottish MacMahon family.

This alone would make a good tale, but it turns out Charlotte's story was not over. I could not relate it any better than the official "Burgundy Today" website so I'll quote it below.

> "Something resembling a French farce then ensued. Louis XVI came to the throne in 1774, and when the French Revolution was in full fling fifteen years later the situation didn't look too good for the old Marchioness Charlotte or her château. Her two sons who had taken up arms with the Revolutionaries, declaring her a traitor, came to Sully to confiscate her belongings. However, old Charlotte sent them packing as she said the house belonged to her. Her sons and their activities were not her problem. Stupid old hag, thought the Revolutionaries, she's bound to kick the bucket soon. We'll come back in six months.

"Six months later, they returned. Charlotte had indeed died. Thanks, however, to the quick-witted estate manager, Claude Beaune, the château was saved. He had placed her body in a trough (in the fireplace of the Grand Drawing Room) and filled it with local brandy. When the Revolutionaries appeared, her body was whipped out of the trough, dried off, propped up in bed with a lace mop cap, the curtains drawn. Everyone went around speaking in whispers saying the Marchioness wasn't at all well this week and the Revolutionaries would do better to come back at a later date . This routine was repeated until the Revolutionaries gave up, and so the château was saved from destruction."

One day I was hiking up the side of the hill from the small town of Baubigny heading for a neighboring village. It had been another beautiful fall day. I rounded a bend high on the trail and right in front of me were the ruins of a medieval town called Dracy. High up in the forested area of the hills, it was inhabited by Burgundians from the 7th to the early 14th century- only 700 or so years. A nearby spring is probably what attracted them to this place...or maybe it was the view. Historical records indicate that, around the time of the Hundred Years War, "dangerous mercenaries" (a middle-ages version of a "gang") burned the town's homes. All that remains now are the stone footings that outline the buildings. As I moved on my way I thought to myself, "My ancestors could have lived here." After all, I am said to be a direct descendant of Charlemagne!

If you think that is old, just wait. Driving through the countryside, we saw a sign outside of one sleepy little burg that said *Colonne Romaine* with an arrow pointing down a side road. Following the signs as we often do, we drove down a path that ended in a farmer's field. There, in this bucolic setting, stood a Roman column carved of stone. It was erected to commemorate a great battle that was won in the area. Measuring about 15 feet tall and two feet in diameter, it dated from the 3rd century CE. Now, that's old! The earth around it had to be excavated down about two feet to get to the original base upon which it stood. I hoped the nearby cows appreciated the history they had in their pasture. This column was another hidden treasure in beautiful Burgundy.

The Burgundian city of Autun boasts several gates also built by the Romans, some with parts of water viaducts still on top. The stones of the gates had intricate carvings and details which are now showing their age. Experts believe they were built in the 1st century CE.

On the outskirts of Autun and built into the side of a local hill sits a Roman Amphitheater. It seats several thousand people and also dates from the 1st century CE. We thought it was good humor (& practical!) that the citizens of Autun had built the school's soccer field and track where spectators could sit in the old amphitheater to watch events. They also added a stage where they can hold concerts and theater performances in the summer. We have enjoyed picnic lunches on the centuries-old steps of the amphitheater, where there are no tourists, no security guards, no fences and no signage.

On the outskirts of Autun stands the remains of a building that pre-dates the Roman occupation of the area. It is called the Temple of Janus, named after a popular Roman deity. This name, however, only came to the structure in Roman times. Various experts have tried to determine its origins and reason for being. No one really knows why it was built, but only that it was constructed a very, very long time ago.

One day we visited the remains of the ancient Gallo-Roman city of Bibracte, which is about an hour from our village. There is a massive archeological dig going on there. They have a wonderful museum, and you can hike around the many acres from site to site. This city of 8,000 inhabitants existed during the 2nd and 1st centuries BCE. Julius Caesar even spent one winter here. In the span of thirty years at about the time of Christ, however, everybody moved out of Bibracte to go to the trendy new town of nearby Autun, mentioned above.

It amazed us how open and accessible to the public this site was. Not only do we never find archeological digs of Roman ruins back in the States, but, even if we did, we wouldn't be trusted to wander around them with no security guards to keep us away from the sites. Anyone could crawl around the Bibracte dig sites, and everyone we saw doing so was very respectful of the place. Pretty amazing.

France has quite a few caves. These alone would not matter to most folks. What is in them, however, is fascinating. I am speaking of cave paintings made by prehistoric people who lived in what is now France. The word "painting" may be misleading as it is believed that the artists would often put the pigments in their mouths and would blow them in patterns and drawings on the walls. Whatever their methods, they captured movement and grace in their artwork.

These ancestors of ours lived well over 25,000 years ago. For reasons that can only be speculated at, they would go deep into the caves to paint their scenes. Since they were primarily hunters, they often painted the game that surrounded them. Using black, gray and ochre, they depicted bison, antelope, elk and bear. And, rarely, they would put their own hand against the cave wall or ceiling and blow pigment at it, leaving an outline.

Over the past century or two, more and more of these cave paintings have been discovered. Sadly, visitors to many of the caves polluted the paintings with soot from torches they were carrying to view them. Today all of them are tightly protected. It is still possible, however, to walk back in time with a guide to see them.

Writing about all these really old things has made me feel younger with each line I have put to paper. So, if you are feeling your age, travel to someplace with lots of things that are older than you. After all, age is a frame-of-mind, and "old" is relative.

23- Being a Student (Joni)

Learning a second language, especially as an adult, is a challenge. For me, it is a challenge that I enjoy immensely. I love how difficult it is, I love the feeling of accomplishment when a French person understands me. I love when I've learned to incorporate new vocabulary into my conversations. Since college, the work involved in learning a second language has given me frustration and joy simultaneously.

I have been taking classes at the Alliance Française of Minneapolis for many years, as time has permitted. In my classes there, I have improved my command of the language in a fun and inviting atmosphere. I decided I wanted to try studying French in a more immersive setting, and this involved registering for a class in France. I've done this twice, and what follows is an honest assessment of how that went for me.

Paris

I signed up for what I thought would be a one-week session at the Alliance Française in Paris. What could be more wonderful than being a student in the most beautiful city in the world? I had to take a placement test online, and then I was assigned my class. We rented an apartment through Airbnb for one week, about a twenty-minute walk from the school. The apartment was typically Parisian, in a Haussmann-designed building with a sandstone façade, a mansard roof and small balconies off of both the kitchen and the living room. It was very small, but for one week it was perfect. The neighborhood was residential: not a shop with Eiffel Tower key chains for blocks. There were several small restaurants, frequented by locals, in the area, and of course there was a bakery just two blocks away. On my walk to school I passed the large Montparnasse Tower, with its bustling commuter train station, as well as a branch of the famous department store, Galleries Lafayette. I walked past two schools, where young children were headed, some of them running frantically so they wouldn't be late. They certainly seemed more concerned about their tardiness than are students at the Minnesota school where I taught!

Upon my arrival for the first day of class, I had butterflies in my stomach. The other students seemed to be much more comfortable entering the school. They had their books and they knew where they were going in this large stone building. Had I missed the memo? I reported to the office, and was given my membership card and my textbooks. I was told what classroom to go to, and I was on my way. The class met on the second floor, so I took the dramatically large stone staircase up one flight, and wandered down the hallway, past many classrooms. Eventually I found mine. I met my teacher, who was working to get ready for class, and she seemed very nice, although I found her difficult to understand. One by one the other students entered, and they obviously all knew each other. I felt very much like a fish out of water, especially since the other students were, for the most part, younger than my own children.

What I learned from the man seated next to me (who was from Taiwan) was that although people come and go (like what I was doing), for the most part, our class consisted of people who were taking French in order to get to the level where they could go to a French university (this is called level B2, or in some cases, C1). The students in this class were preparing to take their B2 test the following week. I had joined them in the 12th week of their studies together. Of the twelve students in the class, about half of them were fresh out of high school. There were also students who were just out of college, and there was one young man- the only other American- who was spending the year traveling with his wife and their young son. All of these students were in this class for four hours every morning, and they clearly spent their afternoons studying. Well, all but one. *Moi.* There was a young lady from Argentina who didn't show her face until Wednesday, although she had been in the group for several weeks- she had been sent there by her employer, and she didn't appear to be particularly engaged in the process. There was a young man from Brazil who showed up late every single day. The teacher in me wanted to scold him.

In addition to the countries listed above, there were students from England, Hong Kong, mainland China, Serbia, and Switzerland. I was accustomed to being in a class with other Anglophones, and I found it very difficult to understand some of the other students. Although their command of French vocabulary and grammar was good, their accents made it difficult for me to know what they were saying. I shared this with the teacher after class, and she told me to be patient and that it would become easier as time went on. That never really happened.

The teacher was very well prepared for class every morning. We would start out by looking at verbs on her Smart Board, and she would call on us to conjugate verbs in the tense that she asked for. I found this to be very intimidating, but you can imagine that I became highly motivated to go back and review verbs that I had learned years ago. Sometimes we would have teams, and we would take turns competing against someone on the other team to correct the mistakes in a sentence. The just-turned-drinking-age set seemed to enjoy this a lot more than did Grandma Joni! Sometimes we would walk around in two circles, and would be asked to discuss a topic with the person we found walking next to us. I found it very interesting to hear the young lady from China talk about the dangers of freedom.

One morning we had a bit of excitement: the fire alarms went off! Everyone exited the building, and hung out in the courtyard just outside the doors to the building. I have done many fire drills with students over the years, and in all cases it was important to get the students away from the building. That wasn't a concern this time. We were all shoulder-to-shoulder in the courtyard, and many of the students took the opportunity to have a cigarette break. Apparently there was a malfunction of the alarm system, nothing more, and after about fifteen minutes we all piled back inside.

We took a mid-morning break every day, and the other students were very welcoming to me. They showed me the ropes for ordering coffee and they seemed genuinely interested in what brought me to France and to the Alliance Française. On the last night of class, some of them got together for a party and they invited me (I declined). Most of the topics covered that week were a review for me, but there was always new vocabulary to be learned, and the review of the verb conjugations was great for me. Twelve people in the classroom was a lot, so there wasn't very much opportunity to speak, which I found to be a drawback. Some of the students cried at the end of the class on Friday, as they were now moving on to their home countries, to their universities, or to another class that would begin on Monday. I shed no tears. Although I certainly gained from taking the class, I found it difficult to be so much older than the rest of the students, and also felt I had, for the first time in my life, learned what it is like to join a class where everyone else already knows each other- my heart goes out even more to students who have to pick up and move to a new school mid-year.

Sancerre

Based upon the recommendation of a friend, my second experience at a French school was in the lovely town of Sancerre. Sancerre is a medieval hilltop town in the *Cher* department of Central France, surrounded by vines. With a population of about 1600, it is large enough to have a grocery store and restaurants, but small enough to enable a person to learn one's way around quickly. The town has many narrow, winding streets that open onto small open spaces, or *places.* The largest *place, la Nouvelle Place*, has several restaurants, cheese shops and wine tasting rooms. The most famous thing about Sancerre is its white wine, made with the Sauvignon Blanc grape. The second most famous thing is the cheese made in the neighboring farms, called *crottin de Chavignol.* These *crottins* are discs of cheese about the size of a hockey puck, and you can get them when they are a day old, two days old, or one week old. They are absolutely delicious, and fortunately for us, the wine and cheese go quite well together, making it easy to celebrate life in Sancerre!

The school, Coeur de France, is located at the top of one of the curvy roads of the town, and is in a converted sixteenth century château. Most of the people who study there also rent an apartment from the school, but we chose not to do that, as we were staying in the town for three weeks and my class was for just one of those weeks. Our apartment was a five-minute walk from school: uphill on the way there, a relaxing downhill stroll on the way back. Unlike my walk to school in Paris, I tended to see the same two or three people each day, who were standing in their doorways. Because the town is very accustomed to struggling French students wandering the streets, the townsfolk are very friendly, and are very patient with those who are just starting their studies of their language. Every day as I walked past my neighbors, they were happy to respond to my "bonjour, monsieur" with their own "bonjour, madame," which was a wonderful way to start my day.

I was not going to have any classmates at all this time around. This is a much smaller school than the one I attended in Paris, and we were there in late October, when fewer people were interested in traveling to Europe. Because of this, there was no one else at the school at my level, so I opted to take a private class for five days. This consisted of four hours per day for five days. My instructor was a wonderful young man, Fabrice, who had experience teaching languages at the university level and who wasn't shy about expressing his opinions as we compared our countries, discussed American politics, religion and pretty much anything else you could imagine. We would converse for a while, and then he would take the time to go over my mistakes. He would prepare short lessons addressing issues he had noticed in my French. I had homework every afternoon. I gained tremendously from his instruction.

We would take a break mid-morning, and during that time I could visit a bit with the others students at the school. The majority of them were in my age range, or at least closer than they were in Paris. Many were from Australia, some others were British or American, and I also made friends with a woman who was Brazilian but living in Canada. Unlike me, most people were taking classes for two or three weeks. For some, this was the beginning of their language journey, and they were starting at square one. For others, they had been studying for years but now wanted to take their studies to the next level. Everyone was exceedingly friendly, and many times during our stay I would get together with other students for lunch or a glass of wine later in the day.

The school offered optional activities in the afternoon, and they allowed Chip to join us as well. We didn't take part in all of the activities, but we did participate in a few. We went out to a winery and learned about the ins and outs of Sancerre wines (and did not leave empty handed, of course). We also went out to a goat farm and learned about making the Chavignol goat cheese that is so famous and so delicious. Naturally, we had cheese in hand when we headed home. The school also did a happy hour for us on our first evening, so that we could get to know each other.

As I mentioned earlier, we stayed in the town for three weeks, because we had never visited this area before and we wanted enough time to explore and to get to know it. When I realized that the norm was to study for two or three weeks, I wished that I had signed up for more. The owner, Marianne, agreed to give me three more lessons over the course of the two weeks, each lesson lasting an hour. She was an intense but exceptional teacher, drilling me over and over again with vocabulary and verb conjugations until she was certain I had the words and concepts permanently etched into my brain. I love language study because I love being pushed. Therefore, I loved every minute of it.

What a contrast between the two schools! Both schools did good work, but for me, Sancerre was the best fit by far. Although I love Paris, living in this picturesque little town for three weeks enhanced the experience, and I really felt a part of the school and of the community.

24- All That Jazz (Chip)

The French love jazz. I would hazard a guess that today it is more universally embedded in their society than ours. At first, this seemed odd to me. Most of us would say that jazz had its origins in the United States, and is more of a uniquely American idiom. It does not take much reading, however, to see how the popularity of jazz came about in France.

Jazz's first mainstream influence in Europe came after World War I. The large number of GIs on the continent- particularly in France- brought their American tastes in music with them. Once introduced, jazz flourished in France in the 1920s and 1930s. A number of Black jazz musicians, facing racial bigotry in the United States, went to Europe where they were appreciated for their artistic abilities. Jazz greats with names that we might not recognize (Sidney Bechet, Josephine Baker, Bud Powell and Charlie Parker, to name a few) all lived in France during this period. Some of Paris's most famous jazz clubs also got their start during these decades.

It did not take long for France to develop its own very talented jazz artists. The 1930s saw the first two of these greats- guitarist Django Reinhardt and violinist Stephane Grappelli- emerge from the shadow of their American counterparts. During World War II, American jazz musicians were banned in Paris (and all of France) by the occupation Nazi forces and their puppet Vichy government. This was not true, however, of French jazz musicians who, in spite of this horrible time in world history, further developed their own unique jazz styles.

What started with a trickle of jazz introduced during World War I became a flood after World War II. More and more, the French embraced jazz music and musicians in their culture. It could be argued today that Paris might rival New Orleans as the world's jazz hot spot.

"All very interesting," you say, "but what does this have to do with the current narrative?" As musicians ourselves, Joni and I always look for concerts and other musical events to attend while we are on vacation. This was true of our time in France as well.

Many of the vineyards in the area hold open houses in the fall to celebrate the end of the harvest, and the release of a new vintage of their wines. We noticed fliers posted around town for one such event at a place very close to where we were living. It might not have attracted our attention more than any other except that it said "Night of Jazz" on it. This piqued our curiosity. We became even more interested when our friend Juliette told us that the vineyard offering the jazz night belonged to her parents. She encouraged us to attend, as we could also taste many of their wines. On the designated mid-November night, we bundled up against the wind and rain that had been coming down all day, and walked down the street to the event. The mist hung in the air around the streetlights.

We knew we were close to the correct address when cars began lining the street. There were also buses that had driven groups of wine enthusiasts from Beaune for the event. We entered the courtyard and the tent they had erected as a ticket booth. Like many such tastings, they asked for a small donation at the door. For that we received a glass to take around the cellars for tasting, snacks in the cave and a jazz concert. Quite the deal!

As we followed a line of people down into the cellars, we noticed the change in temperature. The constant 60-65° was welcome heat on this chilly night. We wound our way through several caves and sampled many of the family's wonderful wines, both the white and red varieties. One interesting display they had in the cellar was a wine barrel where the wooden ends had been replaced with Plexiglas. From the far end of the barrel, a light shown through, allowing us to see the young wine inside. Tiny bubbles of gas were still being released as yeast did its job of converting sugar to alcohol.

We arrived in a large room that contained the vineyard's primary fermentation tanks. Tonight, however, it had been converted into "party central." Appetizer trays of cheeses, fruits and meats were laid out on a long table. A wide variety of the family's wine was being served. And nearby we heard music playing.

Taking our wine and snacks with us, we followed our ears and found the music. An adjacent room had been converted into a miniature jazz club, complete with staging, theater lights, and a sound system. Benches had been added for seating. A couple of hundred people were sitting around enthusiastically listening to a unique jazz quintet of flute, three guitars and acoustic bass. Surprisingly, the audience was not socializing as I have often witnessed at home, but instead were quiet and attentive.

When the quintet finished its set, everyone took the opportunity to replenish their wine and snacks. The stage was changed over to accommodate a quartet of tenor sax, piano, bass and drums. When these guys got cooking the audience grew larger. We saw several people we knew from the village in attendance. We never would have pegged them for jazz fans but there they were. The pianist and bass player were particularly talented and really in sync with each other. Joni was translating what was being said between numbers for me, and we found out that the pianist had actually written a number of the songs that were being performed.

We stayed through two sets by this talented group. After thanking our hosts and saying good-bye to Juliette we walked through town to get to our late dinner reservations. Over our meal we talked about what a culturally unique situation we had just enjoyed. We could not imagine a local company somewhere in Suburbia USA or farm in Smalltown, Minnesota opening its doors after closing hours to the public, offering samples of its product and enticing that number of people to show up by sweetening the offer with a night of jazz music.

Another French jazz experience occurred in the small town of Saint-Romain. Whereas our village boasts a population of close to 2000, Saint-Romain numbers 250 or so. We had been in this *ville* a number of times on walks, to visit vineyards and to see a barrel-making factory. One part of the town is situated in its own little valley while the other, *Haut Saint-Romain*, is built on a high promontory overlooking a large area. This high village was once the location of a fort that offered military protection to the region.

As picturesque and peaceful as Saint-Romain is, the last thing we expected was to see posters put up around the area advertising an evening of jazz there. Called *Jazz à déguster* (A taste of jazz), it was to feature a trio of musicians. Further reading also explained that, not only would this be a concert, but a sit-down multi-course dinner as well. It was being promoted by the *Musique à Saint-Romain* society. A music society in Saint-Romain where the population was 250 people??? Indeed, this was piquing our curiosity. Joni made a call to the number on the flier, and after some discussion, was able to reserve two seats for the Saturday night festivities.

The event was scheduled to start at 8:30 p.m. Around 8:00 we loaded ourselves in the Peugeot and set off. By this point in our trip I had logged a lot of kilometers driving around the area- even at night. It had been foggy all day and, by the time we left in the dark, it had thickened and settled in for the night. We could see only a short way in front of the car. I carefully routed us through several small villages and the countryside, and onto the road to Saint-Romain.

Although I had driven this particular road many times during the day, I was not prepared for what it would be like at night and in the fog. When you drive around the countryside in the states, even though you are between towns, you do see occasional lights at farmhouses or other buildings near the road. Here, once we left our village behind it was pitch black in the countryside, without a light in sight. This is what happens when the homes are in town instead of near the crops. A very eerie feeling. We did not see another car until we swung into Saint-Romain.

We found the *Salle des Fêtes*, which during the day was part of the local elementary school, and pulled into a nearly empty parking lot. As we parked another car pulled up beside us. Apparently as skeptical as we were about the lack of cars, the gentleman asked if this is where the jazz event was being held. We said we thought so and all walked in together.

Inside we found several locals at a ticket table. We gave our names and were told to go up the stairs to the top floor. We were to be seated at table 8. Led by one of the hosts, we trucked up three flights of stairs to a large room that doubled as the school's gym. On a stage at one end, the musicians were doing a final sound check. Temporary theater lighting had been set up. Round tables, which each held eight people, filled the room. They were set up with linen table clothes and enough silverware to feed an army. As usual, we were the first to arrive.

Within a short amount of time, however, the hall started to fill up. As folks arrived at our table, we greeted a couple from Beaune who were local musicians themselves, and two women from the nearby town of Pommard. Rounding out our group was a plumber, his wife and son. The son studied piano with the keyboard player in the jazz trio we were to hear that evening.

After introductions and a first toast with...what else...Saint-Romain wine, we began a lively question-and-answer session that lasted pretty much throughout the meal and between jazz sets. They, of course, were very curious about how two Americans ended up at this event. We, on the other hand, had many questions about the jazz group that was performing, the regularity of events sponsored by the *Musique à Saint-Romain* society, the dinner, etc. Thanks to Joni's French language skills, some shared bottles of wine and the English they spoke, we were all able to carry on nicely.

The lights dimmed and a MC welcomed everyone, spoke about the various dinner courses, introduced the guest chef from a well-known restaurant in the area, and thanked the musicians and everyone for coming.

The jazz trio of drums, keyboards and trumpet turned out to be colleagues who taught together at a music school in Beaune. After just a song or two it was obvious that they were very experience jazzers. They performed a mini-set between each course of the dinner. During those times, the lights would dim; we would all sip our wine and listen to the music. Then, when the next course was ready, up came the lights, another bottle of wine would be opened at the table and we would strike up our conversation again. I began calculating that, at this rate of time and the number of courses announced at the beginning of the event, we would probably be done just in time for breakfast.

The folks at our table represented a wide variety of ages and professions, yet they all spoke knowledgably about the music, wine and food. We were amazed at a lively discussion that came up at one point about one of the local cheeses served in the cheese course. Although not identified with a sign or wrapper, they all knew exactly what type of cheese it was and who had made it. The discussion was about whether the taste had significantly changed during the past five years due to differences in milk supply, equipment or other factors. And, although we still had bottles of white wine unfinished at the table, the French folks decided that this cheese must be eaten with a red. We just thought it was yummy.

Finally, the dessert course arrived. We stayed around for one more jazz set, and then said our good-byes to our new acquaintances. I'm not sure what time we got home but I am sure it was in the wee hours of the morning.

Not every jazz experience we had in France was totally positive. One day, while strolling through a local town, we ran across a restaurant that advertised live jazz music on the weekends. Having had two recent successful jazz experiences, we decided on-the-spot to make some reservations for the following Saturday evening. We asked what time the music started and were told 8:00 p.m. We arrived at the appointed time and- you guessed it- were the first patrons in the restaurant. In the corner of the room a tenor saxophone player was warming up. He did not sound great but I thought he would get into the swing of things when the rest of his group arrived.

We ordered *Kir* and perused the menu of seafood specialties. Suddenly we heard a blues background of piano, bass and drums start and, after the first few bars, the saxophonist joined in on a lead line. It turned out he had not been waiting for the rest of the group; he *was* the group. He was using canned music from his laptop computer to accompany himself. This alone would not have been too bad but he was terribly out of tune and did not seem to notice it. It was pretty painful.

By this point more patrons were arriving. We ended up sitting next to a couple from Texas. As conversations began from table to table we realized that almost the entire room we were in was filled with Americans. Later we realized that the French locals, knowing from prior experience that this particular saxophonist was not the best of jazz musicians, had requested tables in an adjoining room of the restaurant farther from the music.

I kept glancing over at the tenor sax player wondering if he would mind if I offered to help him get in tune. His appearance struck me as familiar but I could not quite place the face. Finally, it dawned on me. I turned to Joni and said, "He looks like a long-lost brother to Captain Jean-Luc Picard." (Picard was played by actor, Sir Patrick Stewart, on the Star Trek "Next Generation" series.)

With the exception of the saxophone player, we have had many wonderful nights listening to French jazz musicians. If you travel to Paris, it would truly be a shame if you did not take one night to visit a local jazz club and take in the scene. Whether you want the most contemporary jazz, Gypsy Jazz (*Jazz Manouche*) or jazz standards, there is something for everyone. It is a cultural event you will not soon forget.

25- Barrel Making...with Japanese Tourists (Chip)

Early one morning as I was drinking my coffee, I looked out the window into the courtyard of our apartment home at the winery. It was another beautiful day with a clear, blue sky. I noticed that, across the way from our apartment, something interesting was taking place. Christian was helping a couple of gentlemen set up tables, displays and tools that looked like they would be used for making barrels. As I watched, a small van drove up and a group of Japanese tourists disembarked. Their guide led them over to the barrel folks. Apparently, a lecture/demonstration in barrel making was going to take place right across the courtyard. Nothing even remotely this exciting ever happens at home in Minnesota when I look out the window in the morning- just a few squirrels running around the yard. Since my curiosity was piqued, I grabbed my camera and hurried down the stairs to ask Christian if I could join in on the fun. After clearing this with one of the guides he gave me a thumbs-up.

There were two barrel makers- also known as coopers- on site. One was playing the part of narrator by explaining the whole process. Luckily for me the explanation was being presented in English and not Japanese. The barrel master himself did the demonstrating. As I approached the group, the master cooper was lining up staves inside a metal hoop, the type that you would find on one end of a barrel. He deftly held everything in place with something that must have been akin to the Jedi force. He then took a large hammer and, quicker than twenty tourist camera shutters clicking, he drove the metal hoop down onto the staves, locking them into place. At that point he had an item that looked like a barrel at one end and a crown roast at the other. It all looked extremely easy.

We were divided into teams and each group was given 10 minutes to match the master's barrel. Each team had one of the pros to offer guidance.

"Go!" While one person held the hoop, another fed pre-cut staves into it. A third person tried to hold the staves in place. It seemed that every time a stave was put into place, three more would fall out. In no time at all, barrel staves were falling on the ground. And we were also falling on the floor because we were laughing so hard. The groups finally got to the point of driving the hoop down onto the staves. More laughter and camera shutters greeted our sadly misshapen barrels. Thankfully, time was called. None of us would be making barrels for a living anytime soon.

A trip to the *Musée du Vin de Bourgogne* would further my wine barrel education. A wine museum might seem a bit boring to some folks but, to me, it was very interesting and was a chance to learn more about my favorite hobby. I saw tools that had been used for centuries in the winemaking industry. Surprisingly, they were very similar to some of the tools I had seen in use at "our" winery.

Some experts actually speculate that the first barrels were made in Burgundy itself. Although no one knows for sure, it is thought that the shape of a barrel is such that it makes it easy to roll on and off ships. Other more far-fetched theories say that they are like an egg with the ends cut off because the egg is where life begins. What this has to do with wine making beats me, so I'll go with theory number one.

However it came into being, the shape of a barrel makes its construction particularly tricky and fascinating.

A video at the museum showed coopers making barrels using only traditional methods and hand tools. (Have you noticed how "traditional methods" usually translate into "slow and tedious?") It showed the oak staves being cut to length, shaped concave on one side and convex on the other. The staves are then carefully tapered at each end, based on a pattern. Taper them too much and the barrel leaks; too little and the barrel will not come together enough for the hoops to fit. Additionally, each barrel has three widths of stave that must be inserted in a specific pattern. (I *know*; exciting stuff, isn't it?)

After the traditional cooper makes the crown roast beginnings of a barrel I described above, it is then time to heat and steam the wood. A small fire is made using the scrap ends of the staves. The crown roast end of the barrel is placed over the fire and water is carefully applied. The steam softens the wood and makes it more pliable. When the cooper determines that the staves are ready, the bottom of the barrel is pulled together using a rope and a large turn screw. A typical finished barrel has six metal hoops. Some barrels also have up to eight wooden hoops made from chestnut trees. These chestnut hoops are really just to protect the oak when the barrels are rolled around. (Just as an aside-after tasting roasted chestnuts in France, I personally don't think that "chestnuts roasting on an open fire" taste very good. Just trying to save you money.)

After crafting the barrelheads out of oak planks, the traditional cooper inserts them into his empty barrel and drives them into place in a groove he has cut to hold them at each end. He finishes by tightening the hoops and drilling a hole to use for adding wine. *Voila,* a finished barrel after only one very, very long work day.

Back in the courtyard at the winery, our narrator explained how the fire and heat also toasts the inside of the barrel. This toasting allows flavor from the oak to be absorbed by the wine. A light toasting takes one hour over the flames, a medium toast 90 minutes, and a dark toast takes two hours. The darker the toast, the more flavor is imbued into the young wine. Vintners will order barrels based on the forest from which the oak was harvested and on their particular desires for the amount of toasting. Some will go so far as to employ different toasts depending on the condition of the grape harvest on any given year. It is estimated that a finished barrel imparts 50% of its flavor in the first year of use. Each succeeding year is about 50% of whatever flavor is left.

The barrel master told us that, still today, the test for an apprentice to become a master barrel maker is to make a complete barrel from scratch using only hand tools. They must accomplish this within a scant sixteen hours.

Using modern techniques, it is estimated that each craftsman, with the assistance of apprentices, can now make 50 barrels per day. Each barrel costs between 500-800 Euros. That is about $650-$1000 each. Depending on the vintner, a barrel can be used for just one year or several. (If you go to Burgundy and want to view barrel making, go to *Tonnellerie François Frères* in the Burgundy village of Saint-Romain.)

At the end of the demonstration, we were each given a stave of our own from an old barrel. How they expected us tourists to get these home is beyond me...but it's the thought that counts.

Being around so many barrels of wine during our time in France, I got it in my head that having one of these barrels at home in Minnesota would make a great souvenir and conversation piece. I began thinking about how I could get one from France to the states. Some brief research revealed that it would be cost-prohibitive to ship a barrel overseas. I had a middle-of-the-night idea that I could fill it with clothes and tell the airlines it was an extra suitcase. Like most such ideas, it seemed better in the dark than in the light-of-day.

One day, while exploring a nearby town, we were wandering into various antique stores. Suddenly, the answer to my barrel dilemma was there in front of me. Hanging on the wall was a very old miniature barrel. I had seen the same thing displayed at the wine museum. It was called a *tonnelet.* In the 19th century, it was employed by the workers in the fields to hold their daily allowance of wine or beer. It even had the workman's initials stamped into the barrel's lid. Although this one was in rough shape and not a museum piece, it called out to me. And, it would fit into my suitcase!

The little Buy-It-Chip on one shoulder shouted, "Buy it!"

Ah, but then the little Save-Money-Chip on the *other* shoulder said, "Wait a minute, do you *really* need this?"

Buy-It-Chip: "Of course you don't *need* it, but you really *want* it."

Save-Money-Chip: "Don't you need to save money so you can go on more trips like this?"

Buy-It-Chip: "Make Joni save more money for next time."

Save-Money-Chip: "Then there will never be a next time." (Wow, I'm glad I didn't say *that* out loud.)

These two bickered on as I walked out of the store.

A few days later, Buy-It-Chip, with the help of the real-life Joni ("*I don't want to hear another word about a barrel ever again if you do not buy this one.*"), convinced me to go back and get the barrel. I walked into the shop and over to where the barrel had been sitting. Gone?!?!? Nooooooooo!!! As I was frantically glancing around to see if it had just been moved, out from the backroom came the saleswoman holding "*my precious*" barrel. Divine intervention? A very savvy saleswoman with a fantastic memory? I'll never know. I do know, however, that *le petit tonnelet* now sits in a place of honor in our dining room.

26- World War Memories (Chip)

France today is a wonderful, beautiful and vibrant country for tourists to visit. I envy its citizens. Great sights, historic buildings, tasty restaurants and spectacular scenery provide wonderful memories. In cities and villages, however, one does not need to wander about much to find signs of the past that are not such great memories. We sometimes forget that France was invaded during the two major wars of the 20th century and that the French people had to defend their homeland. Reminders of these terrible conflicts will be all around you in France once you move past the typical tourist sites.

Even the smallest *ville* has a war monument honoring its lost sons near the city hall or in a public square. In a nearby village the monument inscription says, "*Gloire à nos héros victorieux qui sont morts pour qui vive la France.*" (Glory to our victorious heroes who gave their lives so France could live.) In yet another small town their monument reads, *"Gloire à notre France éternelle; Gloire à ceux qui sont morts pour elle."* (Glory to our eternal France; Glory to those who died for her.) You get the picture. You might also see a museum dedicated to the resistance, or a plaque honoring the local Jews who were forcibly removed to German death camps.

Often, when driving around the country, we will come upon a monument to a battle or a significant war event just sitting in the middle of a field or next to the road. In Alsace, we followed small signs that led us through the vine fields to a military graveyard and monument. Row after row of small crosses and stones stood in testimony to the soldiers who had died in battle during World War II. Nearby, the Stars & Stripes still flies over a tribute the French had erected to honor the American soldiers who died to help liberate their country.

In another chapter, we wrote about several historic caves we had visited to see ancient cave drawings made by our prehistoric ancestors. More recently, however, many of those caves were used as hideouts for French resistance fighters during World War II. They would store munitions and supplies in them, and sometimes would hide crashed American and British airmen who they were trying to rescue.

The old Romanesque church in Semur-en-Auxois was deserted on the late fall day that we visited the city. I had wandered through many churches during our stay that were much more spectacular than this one. It had, however, been raining during our visit to this town, so we decided to go in and take a look around. As I was taking it all in, my eye was drawn to a small side chapel just to the left as we entered the nave. There I saw a stained-glass window that depicted several United States World War I soldiers in the midst of battle. Below it was a plaque in both French and English that read-

IN MEMORY

of the dead of the 310th infantry 78th division

United States Army who fell in the Great War

1917 - 1918

and of whom the greater part rest in France.

The memory of two world wars looms large in France. As we drove or hiked through small towns, we could not help but think of all of the war movies we had seen, with American GIs carefully entering small French villages searching for and fearing the enemy. Frequently we could see buildings that had bullet holes in their sides. As we hiked through the Burgundy woods, we thought about the resistance fighters who may have been hiding amongst the trees, or in nearby barns or farmhouses.

During World War II the area of southwest France around Oradour-sur-Glance had a large French resistance contingency. In June of 1944, shortly after D-Day, resistance fighters had captured a high-ranking German officer. The commander of the 2nd SS-Panzer Division stationed in the area had heard from French Vichy Government informers that the officer was being held in the village of Oradour. On June 10, he sent in his troops to surround the town, free the officer and make reprisals against the citizens.

Although the officer was not found in the town, the German soldiers rounded up all the citizens. They confined all the women and children to the local church. The men were put into several buildings around the town. The Germans then began gunning down the men, often shooting them in the legs so they would die slowly. Once the shooting stopped, the Germans doused the buildings with gasoline and burned them, often with men still alive inside.

The soldiers then moved on to the church and ignited it using an incendiary bomb. When the women and children tried to escape the fire, they were shot in the churchyard. Ultimately, the Germans burned down the entire town and everything in it. Over 600 inhabitants of Oradour were dead within hours. Although many French towns had seen reprisals for various events during the war, none came close to the horrible brutality of this occurrence.

After the war ended, French President Charles de Gaulle decided that the town would not be rebuilt, but instead would remain in its burned-out state as a memorial to those who had died there. Only the bodies of the dead have been removed.

We had read about this small French town and decided to make a visit. Needless to say, it was a sobering experience. A parking lot fed us into a memorial center that told of the events that occurred on that day. We then exited out the back of the building, down a gravel path and into the former town. At the entrance, a sign simply reads *Souviens-toi* (Remember).

Within the former town, buildings had no wood or ceilings left, but only their stone walls remained. Glancing through openings where windows and doors used to be, we could see the remains within the houses exactly as they had been left when the citizens were rounded up. Pans were still sitting on stoves. A sewing machine sat waiting for its owner who would not return. Hulks of cars and trucks, their tires and windows long gone, sat exactly where they had been burned. Block after block, the stores, the houses, the train station- all were destroyed by fires set by the Germans. The church, in spite of its burned condition, was still recognizable, standing as a memorial to the women and children who were murdered there.

As with places we had previously visited, such as the concentration camp in Dachau, Germany, it was one of the saddest examples of man's inhumanity against man that I have ever seen.

If you would like to know more about life in France during World War II, a very fine television series, *Un Village Français* (A French Village) can be found on various streaming channels (in French with English subtitles).

The French continue to remember and talk about the two world wars fought on their soil in the 20th century. After all, they make a conscious effort to recognize all their history, honor their past, and pass a respect for their ancestors on to future generations.

27- War and Remembrance, A Personal Story (Joni)

From time to time in this book I've mentioned my friend Suzanne, and her husband Samuel. Suzanne is from Belgium with Dutch ancestry. She and her husband are Jewish, which is not common in our village. The first time I visited Suzanne's home, she gave me a tour which included a little room that she and her husband had turned into their "synagogue," as there are none in the area. It was a special little room which I could easily envision as a peaceful place to shut out the world and worship God.

Suzanne is nearly always smiling with a warm grin that could melt any heart. When I saw her synagogue, it reminded me of a question I had for her. Had her family left Holland for Belgium in order to escape the Nazis? I never got the answer to that question, but I instead heard a story that was deeply personal and emotional.

During World War II, both of Suzanne's parents were taken to Nazi concentration camps. Against all odds, both survived.

Her mother found a small hole in the wall of the building she was in and managed to escape through the hole and out of the camp at night. Thanks to the help of strangers, her mother was not recaptured. It is hard to imagine the fear- as well as courage- that this young woman must have had. Any of the people who helped her along the way could have betrayed her. All of them were risking their lives, and the lives of their families, by helping out this frightened but brave girl.

Suzanne's father was taken to a concentration camp along with his two brothers. Near the end of the war, they were on one of the now well-known Nazi death marches to Dachau Concentration Camp in Germany (a camp Chip and I have visited numerous times, as we have taken our Minnesota Ambassadors students there every two years). On this horrible march, if someone fell down or simply stopped to rest, the person was shot and killed. It is hard to imagine these people, weak and starving, seeing their fellow prisoners shot down in cold blood as they marched on to an unknown location and future. One of the three brothers was very ill. The two healthier brothers, weakened and starving themselves, took turns carrying their struggling brother during the march.

Under their living conditions on this march, they were all horribly frail and pencil-thin themselves. As the long trek continued, it became more and more difficult to carry the sick brother even when the two of them carried him together. Eventually, they just couldn't carry him anymore without collapsing themselves. They had to make a horrible choice. The other "healthy" brother explained to Judith's father that they would need to leave the third brother to die or all three of them would be killed. They made the painful decision to leave the weakest brother, who was then immediately killed. Suzanne's father was troubled by nightmares about this for the rest of his life. He would wake up at night reliving the experience of leaving his brother behind. He couldn't get over the decision he had made, in spite of having no choice.

At the end of the war, American soldiers came to Dachau, where Suzanne's father was buried in a huge pile of dead bodies. Most of us have seen old film footage of the American GIs who were, of course, shocked and sickened by what they found. They stood in horror, regarding the bodies before them. After a time, they were about to carry on with their work liberating the camp when one of them said, "Wait! I saw something move over there!" He saw one finger sticking out of a pile of dead prisoners, and he thought he saw it move a little bit. The soldiers went to the pile and dug out the body that belonged to that one weak finger. It was Suzanne's father, left for dead by the Nazis, who was buried beneath other bodies and was making one last valiant effort to survive.

Suzanne's life reflects the lessons taught by her parents and uncles. She is not one to complain. She is not one to be frivolous. She knows how to use every bit of food in the house to make a delicious meal. She won't tolerate waste. As warm and friendly as she is, she also guards her privacy. You won't be finding her on Facebook or other social media. To her, it would be foolish to give out so much personal information that anyone else could find and use. At the same time, she appreciates everything she has and deeply loves the people in her life. She takes nothing for granted. She appreciates what the sick and starving of the world are going through. She could justify leading a self-centered and bitter life. She could be filled with anger. Instead, she is one of the kindest, most giving people I have ever met.

When we arrived in the village for our second stay she brought over bread and homemade jams because she knew that we would need something for breakfast our first morning. She has given me books and has shared DVDs with us to help us improve our French. Like women around the world we sit and share stories about our children and grandchildren, and our different backgrounds don't matter one bit. One day I went over to her place and we sang French songs with karaoke in the living room. Then I insisted we sing some Beatles songs in English (after all, she wants to improve her English, just as I want to improve my French). I can only picture Suzanne with a smile on her face. Like her husband, she is brilliant, and without meaning to, she puts me to shame with her vast knowledge of global politics and current events. I miss her when we aren't in France, and I respect her tremendously. Just don't ever complain to her about your pampered life being tough. She knows better.

28- Shut up legs! (Chip)

As we mentioned in an earlier chapter, we have had a love affair with the Tour de France for quite some time. Often, as we sat watching this cycling race on our television at home, we would say, "Wouldn't it be great to see part of the race in person some day?"

A good friend of ours sent us a text message. She had discovered a place near Carcassonne that was a vineyard, bed-and-breakfast, and restaurant all rolled into one. And...they were offering a Tour de France Package with transportation to-and-from one of the stages starting in a nearby town. Unfortunately, our friend could not make this work in her travel schedule. We, however, said, "Why not?" Uncharacteristically, for two people who plan months in advance, we booked it a day later.

Our plan was this: Book a high-speed train from Paris to Bordeaux. We would spend a couple of days exploring this city. Then we would pick up a rental car and drive to Carcassonne, and see the race the next day. On the way back to Bordeaux, we would do some wine tasting in the Bergerac and Bordeaux wine regions.

We decided we would travel light as we would not be gone that long. Small, carryon suitcases and daypacks- that was it. At the last minute, however, we decided to bring our wine suitcase. This squarish red bag holds twelve bottles of wine neatly separated in Styrofoam tubes. It has wheels and a pull strap. We had used it on one previous trip. It is a little awkward to drag around behind oneself as it has a tendency to bang into your heel every time you take a step. It is by far the best way we have found to safely transport wine through airports and flights. Why not on this trip as well?

We arrived in Paris quite tired. It was brutally hot in France at this time. We made our way to the high-speed train terminal (the TGV) only to find that our train was delayed by several hours. In the crowded waiting area there was little to no air conditioning, and no space to spread out. We took turns napping in hard molded plastic chairs. Not ideal.

Finally our train was called. We had reserved seats so that was not a problem. The wine bag, however, would not roll down the aisle so it had to be carried. And, it would not fit in the racks above the seats. I finally ended up storing it in a luggage area at the front of the car.

We settled in for a high-speed dash to Bordeaux. Looking at our watches and making some calculations, we thought we could still make it to our hotel, unload our bags, and get to a restaurant reservation we had made before leaving. All good.

Suddenly a scratchy voice came over the train loudspeaker. I'm not sure I could have understood it even if it had been in English. I turned to Joni for a French translation. She did not look happy. It turned out that, due to the heat, many trains were running late and the tracks, normally clear for the TGV's highspeed run, were now blocked. We would be making more stops than normal and running with reduced speed. A trip that was supposed to have taken under three hours was now going to last much longer. *C'est la vie.* At least we could catch up on some sleep.

We did eventually arrive in Bordeaux, caught a taxi ride to our hotel, and were still able to get to our restaurant reservation around 9:30 at night. Luckily, the French like to eat late and the place was still packed. For once we were *not* the first people to arrive at a restaurant for dinner.

They next couple of days were spent exploring the beautiful town of Bordeaux. The architecture is much like that of Paris with Hausmann-style buildings lining the street in the main part of town. The waterfront along the River Garonne has been reclaimed from its days as a port with warehouses. Now it is a vast pedestrian park area for the city's residents and visitors to enjoy. In spite of the heat wave, we bravely walked much of the town seeing the various sights, parks, and statuary. We toured the beautiful opera house, and then visited one of the local markets where we also had a delicious lunch *avec vin*.

On our second morning we were off via the local trams to the newly built wine museum called "La Cité du Vin." Located on the river just north of the central city, it is a fantastically modern five-story building that looks a little like someone's foot in a slipper. The foot and toes are covered in reflective metal that picks up the sky and river images. The part going up the calf has an open look with lots of windows for great views of the river and city. At the top, an open-air wine bar awaits those who have worked their way up through four floors of interactive wine exhibits.

After sampling some wine and strolling our way back to our hotel, we got out of the heat for a while, watched some of that day's Tour de France stage, and napped. That evening we walked to another local restaurant that had been recommended to us for their tapa-style menu. It was a fun place with a great vibe, good food and live music. One unique feature was the paper menus that were clipped to old 33 RPM records. As we drank and ate, we discussed our excitement about seeing the bike race live in a couple of days.

It took us about three hours of driving to reach our B&B near Carcassonne. Most of it was parallel to the River Garonne with vineyards showing on the hillsides above the river. We were looking forward to several stops to taste and buy wine on our way back to Bordeaux in a couple of days. A friend of ours in the wine business in Beaujolais had given us the names of several possibilities.

We reached our B&B late in the afternoon. It is run by a couple who met in the Caribbean Islands, married, and then decided they wanted to purchase and run a vineyard/hotel in France. Recently their son and his partner have also joined them. The son has now opened a bar/restaurant on the backside of the B&B with great views over the local hills. They have also begun promoting live music and dinner evenings.

After settling into our room, we were invited to tour the vineyard operation along with the other guests. This ended with sampling lots of their wines in the lounge area before dinner. There were other couples staying from England and one couple from Scandinavia. We all enjoyed a family-style dinner. Throughout the meal, the wine of their vineyard was flowing freely. The host was quite adept at getting each person or couple to talk about their lives, travels, etc. The best part was, when the meal ended, we just had to go down the hall to our room for the night.

Before turning in for the night, we confirmed with the son the departure time to go see *Le Tour* the next day. He picked us up in front of the B&B with coffee and fresh croissants from the local bakery for the drive to the start town. That was a good beginning to our day!

Along the drive he detailed how things would go. Earlier that day, he had dropped his partner off at a spot on the tour route to reserve a spot for us from which to view the proceedings. He gave us a choice: We could either just drive to that spot and wait for the tour to go by, or we could first walk through the town where the riders would have their *départ* to see the doings in town that proceed the race. Then, we could walk out of town along the race route until we found them. We chose to do the latter plan.

As we drove towards the start town we saw that many of the intersections with roundabouts were decorated with colorful bicycles, cutouts of team jerseys, Tour de France logos, etc. The excitement was building.

Our host could not drive very far into the departure town as all the roads were shut down. Would it be a problem finding our way? Not at all! All we had to do was follow everyone else who was walking to the center of town.

As we walked towards the downtown area we could hear and sense the commotion that we knew accompanied the start of the tour each day. It is pretty much like a carnival atmosphere with lots of live music, DJs, celebrity interviews, food stands, etc. It was already exciting to just be part of that hoopla that we only occasionally glimpsed on the TV back home. We wandered through the crowds just soaking in the atmosphere.

We knew we were going to have a bit of a hike to get to our viewing site so we set out walking about an hour before the race actually started on this day. We also knew that, preceding the race riders, there is a parade of floats sponsored by the various companies that support the race and the riders. As we walked out of town, this parade got going. Giant figures of bike riders adorned some of them; huge plastic animals were on others. Even Mickey Mouse from Disneyland Paris made an appearance. Now away from the large crowd at the start line, we would turn and wave at the folks on the floats. They were almost all throwing freebie souvenirs to the folks along the race route. We each got a hat and Joni scored a t-shirt as well. Lots of candy and key chains also came our way. The heat of the day was starting to build. I turned around as one of the final floats approached and waved at the young lady on top. She waved back, and then, instead of throwing goodies, she shot water at us out of a spray cannon. Surprise! It actually was more like a mist and felt very nice in the heat.

We reached the parking area where our host had set up his viewing point. They had ice cold waters, fresh fruit, cheeses and other snacks for a light brunch while we continued to wait to see the riders themselves. Sadly, the gendarme who was also parked there to control the small crowd did not think we should be drinking wine in this area. Our hosts were quite disappointed by this. They told us that the year before at this same spot, the policeman was drinking wine right along with them. Ah, well... This was not going to spoil our day.

Pretty soon we noticed the team support cars start to drive past us. These were followed by some of the medical cars, motorcycles with television cameras on them, and race officials in their red referee vehicles. There must have been at least one hundred vehicles that were involved in some capacity of the race operation. I know because, for some reason in my excitement, I took pictures of many of them.

Now we knew that the racers themselves would be there soon. We got our cameras ready for the big moment. Finally, there was the head official's car and...there! The Peloton of riders themselves. On TV this group often looks like a swarm of angry bees. A sharp point at the front end, gradually expanding to the full group taking up the whole two-lane road. Now I was seeing it up close and personal. 170+ riders came storming into view.

Everyone around us was cheering for their favorite team or riders. I noticed two things as they went past us. The first was that I had no concept of just how fast they would shoot by us. On TV, the cameras on the motorbikes and in the helicopters film as they travel along next to the riders. Therefore, you do not get a feel for how fast they are going. Let me tell you- they are traveling from top speed right from the moment the flag is lowered. I thought I would get to spot some of my favorite riders. Hah! They were so tightly compacted and fast that there was no way I could spot an individual. It was a high-speed blur of color zooming past.

The second thing I noticed was how eerily quiet it was. Yes, the fans around us were cheering as were we. The only noise coming from the riders was a whirring sound. It was the air being pushed aside by their wheels spinning at an incredible rate of speed. I've never heard anything like it before.

And then, just like that, they were gone. Wow! We were all very excitedly talking. I was surprised that I had taken any pictures at all. I did not want to miss the moment so I had focused my phone camera on the spot where I thought I would take pictures. Then I lowered it down and took pictures without looking through the phone because I wanted to be "in the moment" of seeing the race myself. Some of the pics were blurs but others were terrific. I was finally able to spot some of my favorite riders when I zoomed in on my pictures. Even though it was over in moments, it was a big bucket list item to check off my list.

Since we had to wait some time before the road was open, we sat around socializing with our hosts. Finally we were able to get on the road and take a very circuitous route back to the B&B. As we drove and talked, they invited us back to their restaurant for some more late lunch/early dinner and some wine.

The final excitement for the day was saved for when we got back to our room several hours later. On went the TV, and we got to watch the end of the race stage we had seen set out that morning. The riders were still going at full speed for a sprint to the finish line. I could not even imagine how tired they must have been after hours of racing. And this goes on for three weeks, day in and day out, up and down all of France. It brought to mind a saying that one of the riders, Jens Voigt, would write on a piece of paper and tape to his bike each day before he started the race. It simply read, "Shut up legs!"

The next day, before we departed, we bought some wine from our hosts to start filling our wine suitcase for the trip home. Then, as we drove the backroads back towards Bordeaux, we visited several other vineyards and continued to purchase wine to fill up the suitcase.

We finally arrived at the Bordeaux train station to drop off our rental car. We had chosen a hotel near the train station because we had to catch an early TGV in the morning back to Paris. On our drive we were in our nice air-conditioned car. Now, as we exited the train station, the brutal heat of the day smacked us in the face. It was over 100°F. Even though, as the crow flies, our hotel was only a few hundred yards away, we had to circle through a number of curvy cobblestoned backroads to get to it. And we now had a full wine suitcase. I was not used to pulling it around with a dozen bottles of wine onboard. A combination of a long drive, several wine tastings, the suffocating heat, my suitcase, my backpack and a heavy wine suitcase banging into my feet with every step almost did me in. Now I was saying, "Shut up legs!" as we wound our way to the hotel. In spite of this, the whole trip could be counted as a grand success and fun adventure.

29. Small Differences (Joni)

The world gets smaller every day, it seems, and still there are cultural differences between the United States and France. Here are just a few that we have noticed.

As you might expect, most television shows in France are in French, with some German thrown in on a few channels. We do frequently see CNN International and BBC International, so we can get some English language news while in France (or other European countries). The news on these channels, however, is different from ours in the United States, because it takes a world view rather than mostly reporting on what is happening in one's own country. Although the United States does get quite a bit of coverage on these channels, they also broadcast a lot of information about various areas of Africa as well as more in-depth coverage of the Middle East and Asia. We also get weather reports here for Morocco, Dubai and Singapore.

People are polite in France. Much more polite, in my opinion, than back home. When you walk into a shop, you don't just say the French version of "hi." You say, "*Bonjour, Madame*," which translates to "Hello, ma'am." You speak softly in stores, in restaurants and even on the street. You wouldn't want to disturb someone else as that would be rude.

Speaking of rude, let's talk a bit about children. I don't know how they do it. I am the mother of a guy who used to scream "cock, cock, cock" every time he saw a clock in a public space (he hadn't mastered the "cl" sound at this point). If he had been a French child, he wouldn't have done that. I don't know why, but I know for sure it just wouldn't have happened. More to the point, if I had been a French *maman* I somehow would have known how to raise him in a way where he wouldn't have screamed in public places. In France, if there are children in a restaurant, you don't realize it unless you see them. If a child starts to cry in public, *maman* will most likely start walking away, and little Pierre or Lisette will just have to pull it together and catch up.

When I do notice children in restaurants, I see them conversing with the adults or playing games with their phones. No one is going out of their way to entertain them. Also, I see them eating everything the adults eat. I have been told that French children are offered a wider variety of foods at a younger age than are kids in the USA. I see them eating mushroom sauces, snails and a variety of vegetables at an early age. In contrast, when we bring high school students to Europe, we are served chicken with a mushroom sauce in Paris. Many of the students find this to be quite exotic and some of them look a bit frightened!

Dogs are more polite, too. They go everywhere with their owners. Much like the children, if you are in a restaurant, you will probably have no idea that there is a dog at the table (well, beneath the table) next to you.

Not only are the French polite, but they also have been very helpful, friendly and patient with us. I may be wrong about this, but it seems to me that people in France are more likely to be helpful to strangers than are we Americans. I know this goes totally against the stereotype of the snooty French person, but hear me out. I complimented our female Parisian taxi driver on her perfume, and she handed her perfume bottle back to me to try. She told me to go ahead and put some on! Clearly, another cultural difference in this example is that the cab driver had a bottle of perfume in the front seat with her!

Another example would be when we were in Paris with a student group, and one of our high school students passed out on the sidewalk of a busy boulevard in the Latin Quarter. Before I knew it, someone had brought him a glass of water. Another person, unseen, phoned for an ambulance. Another hailed a taxi and offered to ride with me to the hospital. Back in Minnesota, we have something called "Minnesota Nice." I think there is a "French Nice" as well. It is just that the culture is so different from ours, and most of us don't know the rules (let alone the language). So perhaps what I'm really trying to say here is the difference would be the stereotype of the French people versus the reality that we've experienced.

Squirrels. There don't seem to be any. We saw oak trees, acorns and other nuts all over the place when we hiked. We think someone should bring some Minnesota squirrels (preferable the ones from our own backyard) over to sample the good life in France. It would be one of those win-win situations we all look for in life. We stayed at a place called "The Squirrels" the first time we came to France. They told us they had squirrels. We were there for four days and never saw one.

As mentioned in a previous chapter, signage for scenic viewpoints or other points of interest are nearly non-existent. You'll see something indicated on your map, and you might see one sign for it on the road, but then you are on your own. And, sometimes on the autoroute, you see a giant brown sign with an arrow and the name of a point of interest. We have often looked off in the direction indicated for many kilometers, never to spot what was shown on the sign. I have lost all inhibitions about going up to total strangers and asking them in my slowly-improving French where something is. Sometimes they can help me, sometimes it is 30 kilometers away, and sometimes they've never heard of it.

There is a sisterhood of women here, and they feel very comfortable making sweeping generalizations about men. This could be a woman at the bakery, a sales clerk, or basically any stranger you might run into. It didn't matter whether Chip was with me or not. "That's a man for you!" "Why did you bring your husband shopping with you?" "Men! They are all the same!" "He wouldn't understand. He is a man." "He needs to let you decide. Men don't know anything." I always tried to be agreeable, and, of course, Chip waited patiently.

When Halloween arrived during our first fall in France, we did our best to find a pumpkin to carve. We got one at the grocery store, but the largest one we could find was about the size of a small cantaloupe. Chip did a great job carving the little guy, and that night we put in a candle and took it outside for pictures. Because it was the week of All Saint's Day, schools were on vacation. There was a family staying in the other apartment at the winery, across the courtyard. I knew they had a young son, so I went over and asked him if he'd like to see our Jack-o-lantern. He smiled and said, "I have heard about them, but I never saw one in person before!" His dad took pictures of him standing by it.

As the years went by, we saw more and more signs of Halloween in France, mostly at bars. We have heard that businesses have tried to promote the holiday in France, but we have only seen two young ladies in costume in our village, and that was in the afternoon. This holiday has become so commercial in the United States that I personally hope it doesn't catch on in France. And here's another difference: the day after Halloween is All Saint's Day. In France, that means family time and taking flowers to the graves of loved ones. Schools are closed.

You never see kids just hanging out around town. I think they are doing this thing called "homework." Or, since sports and fine arts are not done in schools, the students are with their sports club, or they are at the music school taking private lessons on their instrument. Most of all, I think they are home studying.

High school students don't have part-time jobs. When I do see young people in France, they are almost always with their parents. It is common to see families together on the weekend. I have never seen a person under eighteen in the center of town without family (except on their school lunch breaks, where they are free to leave the building, unlike most American high schools). Never. I've also never seen a teen driving a car, although they can get their learner's permit at as young as 15, provided they have a licensed driver in the car with them. The youngest a French person can be to get their driving license is 18. The letter "A" has to be displayed on the rear of the car for two to three years, and speed limits are reduced for these inexperienced drivers.

You don't very often see the stereotypical male in a beret in France, although I have seen this a couple of times. However, what you do see are older women in skirts, hose and sensible shoes, riding their bicycles around town. No doubt they are headed for the bakery to get their loaves of French bread *("baguettes").* I have heard that until about ten years ago, the average French person ate the equivalent of three baguettes per day. Now that number has declined to one loaf per person per day.

Speaking of bread, in the morning at your hotel you'll be served bread. If you are lucky, that will be alongside some *croissants* and *pain au chocolat*, which is like a croissant with chocolate in the middle. You'll have butter as well as jam available for your bread and/or pastries. For lunch and dinner, you will be served slices of French bread in a basket, but there will not be any butter available for the bread after breakfast.

In the United States, most of us are very accustomed to having all sorts of produce available to us throughout the year. This is not the case in France. For instance, do not expect to find berries after their growing season is finished. When something comes into season, people plan their menus accordingly. One day at the local market, I could tell immediately that leeks had come into season because virtually every woman had huge bunches of leeks in her "*panier*" (the shopping basket they all carry to market). Another week I noticed that every stall was selling endive, and every French woman was buying it. I had only thought of endive as something you'd have in a green salad. Not so! My friend Suzanne was very excited to tell me about her various ways to cook it.

Speaking of going to food markets, shopping at them is something I really miss when I get back to Minnesota. A town's weekly market is quite an event, with people selling things you would expect, such as meat, cheese and produce, and some things you wouldn't expect, such as clothing, knife sets and mattresses. We've even seen a booth full of hookahs a few times. People force you to try their cheeses, olives and sausages. So as not to offend, I always acquiesce. People are baking bread in huge ovens and look like they may have been used in some of those ancient ruins we've mentioned. We haven't tried out a mattress, and we haven't seen anyone hauling one home yet.

Our adventures in the grocery store have been written about in other chapters of this book. But here are some more differences. Chip found something in the store called Heinz "American Sauce." You won't find it in the grocery store at home. It is a combination of mayo, tomato shallots, parsley, the ever-popular mustard, and anchovies. A bit like Big Mac sauce, but not exactly. For your chocolate fix, you can find candy bars filled with liquors such as Kirsch, Williams, Cognac and Limoncello. For research purposes, I found the dark chocolate with Limoncello combination to be inferior to the dark chocolate with Cognac combination. In early fall, you can find school supplies in the supermarket. It was interesting to find a notebook with music manuscript paper in this area. Kids need these notebooks for their music classes in school, where they learn note reading and writing skills. We also saw recorders (the musical instruments, that is) sold in the school supplies section. As mentioned before, you'll see plenty of differences in the meat department. It is really important to know that "cheval" means "horse," for instance. There is also a section for veal and even for bison (country of origin: USA). Every part of an animal seems to be used in this nation. I have chosen to walk past the pigs' feet as well as the beef tongue, even when it is on sale!

At our local butcher/deli in our small town in Burgundy, we've bought ready-to-eat Beef Burgundy, snails and lasagna- no fast food chains in sight, but these were much better takeaway items, in our opinion. Had we wanted to, we could have also bought cow's tongue, breaded pig's feet or a whole rabbit- eyes and all. How about some un-plucked poultry? Maybe next time.

I attended worship services in our village a few times, which was quite moving. The church is a large, stone "Cistercian Gothic" structure from the 15th century with a wonderful organ. The resonance in the space is gorgeous. Aside from the language, and the fact that I don't attend Catholic Mass at home, things all seemed pretty much the same as in an American service, except for one thing. With my mind wandering a bit, I was startled when suddenly everyone, it seemed, was going around kissing one another on the cheeks. What the heck? I quickly looked at the printed bulletin and realized that this was the French version of the "Sharing of the Peace." What was I supposed to do? People were walking all over the place planting their *bises* on each other's cheeks- one side, then the other. I watched this nervously. Was I expected to do the same? Eventually some folks made their way over to me in the back pew. They shook my hand warmly, said, *"que la paix soit avec vous"* (may peace be with you), and moved on. It was quite nice.

30- Casino, Rehearsal, Truffles and a Table (Joni)

On one of our first trips to France, in a town on the Riviera, I asked a local if there was a grocery store nearby. He kept answering me with "Casino- across the street!" I was very frustrated with my French, thinking that the time and money spent over the years had not paid off one bit. How could he have turned my question into a query about where I could gamble? In spite of being very close to Monte Carlo it just didn't make sense.

It turns out that there is a large grocery store chain in France named, you guessed it, "Casino". There are big *supermarché* Casinos in larger towns, and little "*Petit Casinos*" in small towns such as our village. Chip and I have come to judge the quality of a small town by two things: a Casino grocery store and a bakery. If the town has neither of these two things, it is a village experiencing a slow death.

One lovely town that we hadn't explored much until our second fall in the region was Santenay. It is famous for its wines, but a little off the main wine route. I would say this town tries harder- beautiful hanging baskets of colorful flowers line both sides of the bridge into town, and the town square has a large fountain with pretty cafés and restaurants surrounding it. We saw a bakery down the street, but no grocery store. Perhaps we have too much time on our hands on these autumn trips, but because we think it shows how a town is prospering (or not) it has become a point of interest for us. We saw a sign with an arrow that said "Casino de Santenay", but it pointed to the outskirts of town. Hmmmm, we thought, it must be a bigger store than what we have in our village if it needs to be on the outskirts. Good for them. We didn't bother to find the store but were impressed just the same.

Santenay is a town of 800 people, or half the size of our village. A couple of weeks later we decided to take a hike in the area, so parked in the middle of town. As we began our hike we continued to see signs for the Casino, but didn't find it as it wasn't on our hiking route. Three hours later at the end of our hike we entered town from the other direction and there it was.

But it wasn't. Not a grocery store but a real-life actual gambling casino! It was mid-afternoon and there were zillions of cars surrounding the building. Outside, it advertised slot machines, blackjack, poker and baccarat. Other than on the Riviera, I've never seen a casino in France, but that doesn't mean they don't exist elsewhere. In spite of two or three trips to Las Vegas, gambling really isn't high on my bucket list of things to do in Europe, but there it was. We had to make a visit, but the signage at the entrance clearly asked for a certain level of dress. After our long hike we were not only dressed inappropriately but were both a sweaty mess as well.

We came back in the evening a couple of days later, after dinner. The parking lot was empty. What the heck? It was around 9:30 on a Friday night. Inside, we showed our passports to two black-suited men who had a certain "mobbish" air to them- all business, serious and almost threatening looks on their faces. They must have watched a few American movies about Las Vegas to pick up on the appropriate demeanor of a casino employee. After carefully checking our passports, they let us in.

The casino was small by American standards. On the main floor there were about forty slot machines, all seeming to be American, with themes one would see in the states: super heroes, wizards and sorcerers, Cleopatra, Wheel of Fortune, etc.

On the second floor there was a little restaurant with a live band. This was not a good thing. Wherever you went in the casino you could hear this band playing 80's rock music with terrible singing.

On the upper floor were the gambling tables. There were three employees there, sitting in silence...and no gamblers. Chip likes to try his hand (literally) at blackjack, so we sat down. We asked the employees why it was so empty, and they said it was too early. People would start coming much later in the evening, and the casino was open until the wee hours. It is hard to imagine that this would happen in a town of 800 in the USA, but maybe I just don't get out enough to know.

Eventually another man showed up and sat down at the blackjack table as well. At one point, one of the bouncer-type guys came through ("Don't yell at me! I've done nothing wrong!" I wanted to say, as he was so good at looking intimidating.) The bouncer stopped at our table. "Oh, no," I thought, thinking that we weren't dressed well enough, hadn't bet enough money, had somehow insulted *la France*. The other gambler stood up as the bouncer approached, and the two began the kissing ritual that the French do- one cheek, then the other. Seeing this tough dude kissing another man on both cheeks made him lose his tough exterior in record time.

[PS- Much as at casinos in the USA, we lost money.]

Both Chip and I enjoyed long careers as public-school band directors. When we travel, we always see if there is a concert to attend. This is often a town or village band. We have been lucky enough to hear some really fun performances over the years, including one evening where the band performed on a lighted barge in the lake at the edge of the town where we were staying.

It surprised us to learn that our adopted village had its own band. Our friend Juliette plays clarinet in this group, and her father plays saxophone. Friday evenings are when the band rehearses. Knowing that Chip and I were retired band directors, Juliette, invited us to come and see what a rehearsal was like. She introduced us to smiles all around.

In the States, we have school bands of students, and adult community bands, but the two don't often mix. To our surprise, this ensemble was a multi-generational affair, with kids no older than 12 playing along with people who could have been their grand-parents. It was such a cool thing to see. All of the music they were playing had an American flavor: "Ain't Misbehaving," "Stevie Wonder Medley," and a Cuban medley. We can't wait to hear one of their concerts on a future trip. Who knows, we might even join the group!

One crisp morning we headed to another Burgundy adventure. We went hunting for the black gold of France: truffles.

If you aren't familiar with these fungi, they grow just beneath the ground near tree roots. Black truffles sell for a huge price. Burgundy black truffles are going for $225/pound in France. There is an entire illegal business of selling fake, Chinese truffles and passing them off as true French truffles, an enterprise that the French police take very seriously. The truffles themselves are beyond ugly. They are black, round balls with a texture on the outside similar to a Morrel mushroom. Slice one up and add it to eggs, or mince it and add it to a cream sauce. *Voilà*, the taste is like heaven on earth.

Chip saw an ad for a place that takes people along on truffle searches. We made a reservation and headed out early the following morning. We arrived at a barely marked little place out in the country an hour later. We were given our introduction to truffle hunting by the owner of the business. He explained that it is only legal to hunt truffles two ways in France: 1) with a dog or 2) with a pig. These animals need to be trained to successfully hunt. In the case of the dogs at this place, a puppy is fed truffles as a very expensive treat. Then, once it recognizes the scent of truffles, it goes out into the forest with its owner, and runs to find the places where they are growing underground. The dog cannot only smell the truffle beneath the ground, it can tell when it is at the correct maturity to be dug up. The next trick is the hard part- to train the dog not to eat the truffle. We observed all of this in action with the owner's adult son and their six-month old puppy, Julio. Julio was "in training" to become part of the next generation of truffle hunters for the family.

We walked out into a grove of trees that the family planted years ago for the express purpose of harvesting truffles. The man said "*Cherchons!*" (Let's hunt!) to Julio, and off the dog ran. He tore over to a spot about a foot from a tree and started digging for all he was worth. The man quickly got down on his knees, stopped the dog from further digging (and potentially eating) and made him sit. He then took a small digging tool out of his pocket and dug out the little gem, which had a diameter of about an inch. Finally, he dug in his pocket and pulled out a little dog treat. He held the truffle up in one hand while the treat was held up in the other, so the dog could see the two together. Then he fed the treat to Julio and slipped the truffle into a zip-lock bag. "*Cherchons!*" and off Julio went again.

In all, the pup found nine truffles that morning, but his master only received seven of them. Twice Julio was too quick for his trainer and had a nice breakfast snack that no doubt was more satisfying than two little dry dog treats.

When we arrived for our first stay at the winery, we wanted to feel comfortable, as it was going to be a three month stay. Although we had brought a lot with us, we soon discovered that there were some things we were missing. One was a couple of American-sized coffee mugs. Something else we wanted was a small end table on which to place our American-sized coffee mugs while we relaxed in our comfy chairs, checking the news back home on our phones. If we had been back in the United States, we would have gone to the nearest Goodwill store, but these did not exist in France. After some computer research, we found that there was a counterpart in a nearby town, called *Emmaüs.* (Emmaus is an international solidarity movement founded in Paris in 1949 to combat poverty and homelessness.) Off we went.

Although smaller than our American Goodwill stores, Emmaüs was filled with treasures. Not only did we find two coffee mugs, but a perfectly good end table for just five euros. We also found a couple of shirts for Chip, one that had a high-priced label and looked like new. We trundled back to our apartment with our second-hand finds, and made good use of them for the entire fall. Thinking the table and the mugs might come in hand for other visitors to the apartment, we left all but Chip's new shirts when we departed.

The following September we once again arrived at our home away from home, so happy to be back at the winery. Our coffee mugs were still hanging on the cup rack in the kitchen. After searching every room, however, we couldn't find the end table. Finally realizing it was no longer there, we headed back to Emmaüs to find a replacement. Upstairs we went to the furniture area to scope out a new table, and...there it was! Our table had been taken back to the same store where we had originally bought it. So, for another five euros, we again hauled our precious table "home" to our apartment, and all was well with the world once again.

31- Visitors (Chip)

When we first made our plans to stay for extended periods of time in France, we knew we would have friends and family who would want to come visit us. In fact, one of the reasons we picked our apartment in the vines was that it had a second bedroom for guests. We loved inviting these folks into our "home" and showing them around the area that we had grown to love. Here are a few anecdotes about certain visitors that were too good not to share.

Our first guests were Ann, one of Joni's former teaching colleagues, and her husband, Larry. They dropped in for a few days while on their own tour of France. The weather for their visit was very mild for the beginning of October. They are just as nuts about wine as we are so we had a great time visiting small wine towns in the area and sampling many, many wines.

As we were traveling from village to village, we were playing around with the car's GPS. In those days, these were relatively new toys. As we were scrolling through the settings we wondered what the difference would be between the fastest route and the shortest route. I switched it over to the shortest route for the next leg of our journey that day. Suddenly we found ourselves on some of narrowest roads on which I had ever driven. More like a path than a road, it was virtually one lane of ruts running through rolling fields and woods. Luckily, we did not meet another car. From then on, we stuck to the fastest setting instead of the shortest.

We had wanted to visit the town of Vézelay, and thought Ann & Larry would be keen to go as well. We had read about this town constructed on a steep hill with its immense abbey at the top. Originally constructed in the 12th century, the church had been added onto over the centuries. As we approached the town, we rounded a corner in the road, and there, still many kilometers away, loomed the giant abbey on the hill. Quite a sight. One of us had read that the only parking was at the bottom of the town, and that the main street through town was for pedestrians only. We thought, "How steep a walk can this be, anyway?" Well, it was a lengthy and steep climb. The abbey, always in sight like a mirage as we climbed, never seemed to get any closer. Luckily, there were lots of little shops that we could visit when we needed a rest. Finally we reach the massive structure and began to explore. We just happened to arrive as mass was underway. The beautifully sung chants echoed throughout the structure. Five nuns in flowing white habits with ornate "cornettes" (think: the Flying Nun) led the sung liturgy in harmony. We felt transported back through the centuries as we watched and listened to the candlelit ceremony. It was all very moving and made the whole experience more than worth the hike up the hill. Then, as we exited the back of the church, we found a huge parking area that was accessed using a back road to the top. Oh, well. We got our exercise for the day.

We took Ann and Larry to see other sights in the Côte d'Or, and had some wonderful meals at local restaurants. They were the Guinea pigs for all our future guests and, although we have tweaked our "Visitor To Do" list, it remained much the same for future guests.

Good friends Randy and Julie came to visit for a week. In Burgundy, it was that same routine mentioned above- tasting wines, seeing the sights and eating great food in quaint restaurants. We had a great time taking them around the Côte d'Or for three days, then spent another two days with them in Paris.

In Paris we stayed at a lovely hotel on the left bank, near the Sorbonne and across the street from an apartment rented by Hemingway in the 1920s. It was a terrific location with lots of small, winding streets and cafés. Our first evening there, we went to a jazz club and heard a fine quintet featuring Italian saxophonist Stefano di Baptista. Most of the band was Italian, but the guitarist was an American. The club was a small, dark room with chairs set shoulder to shoulder. Except for the four of us, the audience was French and Italian.

The next day we visited the Paris Catacombs, which we had never seen before. In the late 1700s Paris's cemeteries were all full and bodies were being piled up in mass graves. Disease was spreading, and it was decided to move all of the bones from the cemeteries of Paris into these underground quarries. This was all done after dark with a solemn ceremony. The bones were organized in the catacombs according to the cemetery from which they came and the century they were buried. Bones were placed there until 1814. These days, visitors walk for about a mile underground to where the passageways are lined with these bones and skulls arranged in artistic displays. Why hasn't anyone made a horror movie about this place? By the way, just a few months before we were there, three inebriated visitors got lost down there (which you would really have to do on purpose) and weren't found for two days. No thanks.

We also visited the Grand Palais, a beautiful glass-topped building, built in 1897 for the Paris World Fair. It is now a building that houses temporary exhibitions. We were in luck as there was an exhibition of the art collected by Gertrude Stein and her brother, Leo. I knew that she had been an art collector but had no idea that she had a collection this amazing and extensive. We saw room after room of Picasso paintings and sketches, plus many works by Matisse and Cézanne. Continuing with the Hemingway connection, this was likely the artwork that he would have been looking at during his many visits to Stein's apartment in the 1920s. The only downside to our visit was the wait outside to get our tickets. The wait itself wasn't bad but the nearby street musician was. We would have been happy to have given him some spare change if he would promise us to use it for some new clarinet reeds.

Before we left our apartment for Paris, we had been discussing our itinerary with Randy and Julie. For one of our evenings in Paris, we had booked a once-in-a-lifetime meal (translation: really expensive) on the first deck of the Eiffel Tower. This reservation had been made by Joni before we even left the United States. Joni asked me to remind her what night the Eiffel Tower dinner was, and I confidently told her it was the second evening. Perhaps my wife trusts me too much. Hearing my confident response, she never checked the reservation herself, which she had printed out and placed in a folder before we left home..

Fast forward a couple of days. We had spent a wonderful day in Paris and were now looking forward to our special evening meal. As we were getting ready in our hotel room, I got out the reservation papers we were supposed to bring with us. A confused look crossed my face. Could this be correct? *Mon Dieu!* The papers said our reservation had been for the *previous evening*. I explained to Joni what was wrong. After wringing our hands for a minute, we decided that Joni should call the restaurant, explain the situation, and see if there was any remote chance we could come tonight instead. We knew it was a long shot but had to at least try. Joni enlisted the assistance of the woman at the hotel's concierge desk to help her with the call. Meanwhile, I had to come clean to Randy and Julie about the mix up. They were very understanding.

We waited outside the hotel for Joni to appear and deliver the results of her conversation. As soon as she opened the door, I knew she had been successful. Turns out, she had spoken with a very nice gentleman who understood our dilemma. He told us he could get us in, where to go when we arrived, what elevator to take, etc. He even said to ask for him when we arrived. It all worked like a charm. *Merci Monsieur.*

Once we were seated and able to relax, we had a great time. Our meals and wines were wonderful. After dinner, it was fun to wander around on the Tower's first level and see the City of Lights from on high. It was so beautiful with the tower lit up like gold, and with all of Paris below for us to see.

We received an email from my cousin, Cindy. Turns out she and her husband, Lowell, were about to begin a bike trip around France that would take them, not only into our area of Burgundy, but literally past the door of our home. After exchanging a number of emails, it was decided they would stop for a picnic lunch on their way by that day. Sadly, the weather turned damp and prevented us from eating outside but we still enjoyed a nice lunch and some wine, while catching up on their trip and our adventures.

Later that day, they invited us into Beaune, where they were staying, to join them at a wine tasting that had been pre-arranged by their travel company. We met our tasting guide, a young woman from Australia, at their hotel. She had now lived in Burgundy for many years, making wine. She took us on a wonderful and informative tour of the caves in which she worked.

She then asked if we wanted to taste two different wines from the same year, *or* two wines from the same plot of grapes made in different years. We decided on the latter. I jokingly said, "Yes, let's try two bottles of *Grand Cru* wine from two different years." (*Grand Cru* is the most select and expensive wine available in Burgundy.) She just laughed at me.

A couple of minutes later she came up the stairs carrying- SURPRISE!- two bottles of *Grand Cru* wine. She mumbled something about, "Well, these have to get drunk sometime." We had very generous pours of the 2006 and 2009 *Grand Crus*, both of which were superb in their own way. It was actually quite amazing how different they tasted just because of the different growing conditions in a given year and the three-years difference in their aging.

While we were drinking, our host showed us maps of where the grapes had been picked, talked to us about the different growing conditions those two years...and kept pouring more of the wines. As we were socializing we found out that she also works at a vineyard near our apartment, and she actually helped with the harvest at our winery when she first came to Burgundy. After thanking her profusely, we asked for one of her cards so we could get in touch again in the future. I kid you not- Her name was...Jane Eyre.

One of Chip's former colleagues, Chuck, and his wife, Julie, came to visit. We picked them up at the airport in Paris. Although jet-lagged, they were excited to be in France. By now, our drill with visitors was pretty locked down, and we spent three enjoyable days showing off our adopted area of France.

While visiting the Chateau of nearby Rochepot, we saw an old drawing of the tomb of Philippe Pot, who was born there in 1428. Philippe was a very successful Burgundian knight, nobleman and diplomat of the 15th century. At one point in his life, he was given another nearby castle at Chateauneuf that we have often visited with friends.

We knew, from a sign posted at Rochepot, that we could now see a life-size recreation of Philippe's tomb at the Chateauneuf castle. Off we went to view it with Chuck and Julie the next day. His tomb is a very unique and dramatic structure. A life-sized representation of Philippe lies in repose, dressed in full battle armor, his dog at his feet and his hands in prayer. He is being carried by eight fellow knights, shrouded in mourning, to his final resting place. Although the actual resting place of Philippe has long disappeared to history, his tomb was hidden in an abbey during the French Revolution so as to not be destroyed. A sign at Chateauneuf said that the original tomb was now on display in the Louvre Museum in Paris. We all decided that our first mission upon visiting the Louvre in a couple of days would be to find Philippe's authentic tomb.

We went with Chuck and Julie back to Paris for a couple of days of whirlwind sightseeing before they flew home. Tons of fun for them (we hope!) and for us. We always enjoy visiting this beautiful city. Although we had lots to do- visiting *Sacré-Coeur*, a Seine River cruise, drinking the best hot chocolate in Paris, riding to the top of the Eiffel Tower, Chuck trying on green jeans, Julie singing with a street musician in front of the Paris Opera- we also had a mission to complete at the Louvre Museum to find Philippe Pot's tomb.

I looked at the Louvre website and found the wing, floor and room in which the tomb was located. As we entered the museum, instead of turning towards the Mona Lisa with the throngs of tourists, we instead headed for a less-visited area of the museum. This museum contains hundreds of galleries and halls, dead ends, and stair cases galore. Even if you know approximately where you want to go, it is easy to get turned around. It is sometimes hard to grasp the fact that this was a home for the French royals. If you wanted to go visit your sister for the afternoon, you might leave for her wing shortly after breakfast and be back by bed time. After several wrong turns, we finally found the right gallery. There, in all its glory, we found the original Pot tomb. It is really a remarkable monument, and a miracle that it has survived for over 500 tumultuous years. I would highly recommend you check it out if you are ever in this museum.

One fall, my cousin, Marga, and husband, Larry, paid us a visit in France. We picked them up at the Geneva, Switzerland airport. After a yummy and cheesy lunch, we wound our way through a small part of Switzerland and back into nearby France. We had decided to take some back roads so our guests could see more of the countryside and the villages. At one point we were detoured off our main route and through a small village. Suddenly I had to brake the car. A parade of cows coming in for their afternoon milking brought all traffic to a halt. They were not in any hurry to clear the road so we all got out and took pictures.

Although we had cool weather while they were in France, we enjoyed taking Marga and Larry to many of our favorite haunts in the Côte d'Or and Burgundy. One of the activities we had learned that visitors love to do is to visit a typical French market, and purchase lunch for a picnic later in the day.

As we left the market town, we saw signs for a nearby village that was holding its annual Autumn Festival. Even though we had never heard of this town, the size and quantity of signs gave us the impression that this was not an event to be missed. The GPS did its thing, and, as we neared the village, we following signs for parking in nearby fields. Much like parking at the Minnesota State Fair, there were many people waving us to a parking spot with bright orange flags like we were parking a plane at an airport gate. A short walk towards the village led us to the ticket table. We dutifully purchased four entries and were looking forward to a Disney-like afternoon. Well...*that* didn't happen. Instead the "festival" looked more like a glorified garage sale with a few tired looking midway rides thrown in. No treasures were purchased. The one consolation was that the village had some nice new public bathrooms that were free! Unheard of in France. We all made good use of them.

After a nice lunch of goodies we had bought earlier at the market, we toured Rochepot Castle. Since our last visit this castle had been sold. As it turned out, it was purchased by a Ukrainian using a fake French passport. We later read that the owner, who had faked his own death in the Ukraine and had been hiding out in the castle, had been arrested. Europol officials dubbed him "King of the Castle" and said he was involved in a complex case of international fraud and money laundering. At Rochepot Castle they recovered around 5 million in illegal property including fancy cars, expensive jewelry and works of art by Salvador Dali. As we toured the beautiful, serene castle gardens, little did we know that all of this intrigue was taking place within this property.

Our friend, Juliette, invited us all to tour and taste at her father's vineyard. She served as tour guide, showing us around the vines and their wine making operation. Juliette then invited us to lunch at her place which was a real treat for all of us. This "light lunch" was a gorgeous spread of Burgundian cheese, *jambon persillé,* fresh baguettes and, of course, a bit of wine. Juliette doesn't do things halfway.

Early the next morning we started winding our way towards Paris. En route we stopped at a small village bakery for coffee and a snack. We purchased éclairs and went outside to a small table to eat them with our coffee. They were light and fluffy, and stuffed with some of the best chocolate cream filling I have ever tasted. My cousin took her first bite, and a look of sheer awe came over her face. She turned to her husband and said, "Larry, you march right back in there and buy more of these." He dutifully did just that.

Sue, another of Joni's former colleagues, and Marv, her husband, flew over for a week. The usual touring and wine tastings were on the agenda.

One evening, we all decided to have a nightcap drink. After a long day of touring, wine tasting, and a dinner out, we wanted something other than wine. Our friend and *gîte* owner, Antoine, had left a bottle of *Marc de Bourgogne* for us to sample. This seemed like the perfect time. *Marc* is made from the leftovers from the wine production process-grape skins, stems, seeds. It is a high-alcohol brandy-type drink. One of the rules about making it in Burgundy states that it must be must be removed from the copper distillers at no more than 72% alcohol. Yikes!

I got the bottle out and noticed that the bottom was slanted like it was already drunk. Perhaps that should have been our first clue that this was a potent drink. We began sipping it while nibbling on some chocolate. As the evening wore on, the *marc* began to taste better and better. Finally, the chocolate was gone and the *marc* bottle was empty so we all staggered off to bed.

The next morning Sue came downstairs and asked what we had been drinking the evening before. After I reminded her of the name, she said, "Good. I want to remember that so I'm never tempted to drink it again." As Marv later put it, "*Marc* is the kind of drink that, by the time you realize you've had too much of it, you don't care."

32- Fête and Farewells (Joni)

At the end of one of our stays, we wanted to find a way to thank our French friends and neighbors for all of their hospitality. We had been wined and dined by them multiple times throughout the fall and over the years. Not to mention that, as usual, they were always there for us when we needed advice or "how to" help, and we wanted to reciprocate. We invited all of them to our place for before-dinner drinks and snacks.

The evening's food preparation involved a more challenging time in our small kitchen than a meal for two or three people had in the past. Deviled eggs were no problem, as there is never a shortage of mayonnaise or mustard in France. Wanting to present our friends with some American-styled snacks, I also decided to make pinwheel tortillas spread with cream cheese and other goodies that were then sliced into tasty snacks. The hardest part of making the pinwheels turned out to be finding toothpicks to stick into them. After many strolls up and down the aisles of the grocery store, Chip finally found some cocktail toothpicks with colorful plastic whales on the end. Were they for shrimp cocktail? We'll never know. I also took a huge risk and made tiny French popover-like cheese snacks called *gougères*. My anxiety ran high about trying to make this for our French friends, with our French oven that I didn't completely understand, but they turned out great! Our guests seemed quite amazed that *l'américaine* could do this. Other cheeses, meats and chocolates rounded out our snacks for the evening. We served wine from the "backyard vineyard" at the winery where our apartment was located.

It was a warm late-autumn evening. Perfect for our farewell *soirée.* As our friends started to arrive we were quite overwhelmed with just how many folks in this small community had become so important in our lives over the past several years. Many of our guests were also surprised to learn how many people we counted as friends in the village; They knew each other but had no idea that we knew all of them. I would hear them asking one another in French, "What? How do YOU know them?"

People accepted their wine gladly, and were socializing, but the food sat untouched. I had purposely selected nothing but finger food for this event, as our kitchen wasn't really set up for serving a crowd. "C'mon, eat up!" I thought to myself. I finally turned to a friend and asked, "Why won't anyone take any food?" She whispered to me, "They want silverware." *Merde.* I ran to the kitchen, grabbed every single fork we had, and set them out. *Voilà-* our *invités* were at the table *tout de suite*!

Luckily, our apartment had a pretty large living/dining area so there was room for everyone. At one point in the evening Chip and I looked at each other and smiled. We were both thinking about all the friends and all the history in the room, and how anxious we had been before starting this adventure years prior.

It was a very fun evening, but over all too soon. At the end of the evening, even the dogs were invited in, which certainly helped with cleaning up the floor.

When we first told our Minnesota friends that we were off for three months in a French community knowing not a soul, they thought us very brave. Many of our acquaintances followed our blog, awaiting to see what would befall us. Would we have regrets? Would we be anxious to come home, wishing we had gone for less time? Would we end up hating the experience, craving fast food and American television? That first fall in France, we posted our blog entries once per week, and could see that people were not only reading our posts, but were sharing them with others.

By the end of our first three months in France, life seemed very normal to us in our new home. We were not at all in a hurry to get back home, except, of course, to see our family...and to use our own washing machine. One evening, before the end of our first stay, Chip said, "We must come back here. I cannot stand the thought that this is the end." Turns out, I was thinking the same thing. It was not long after we got home from our first stay in France that we began planning the next trip for the following fall.

We have taken many typical tourist trips- one or two nights in a town, rushing from one museum to the next, then repeat the drill for two weeks until you are exhausted. We still take trips like this occasionally. We have found, however, that we now prefer a much more relaxed pace, and enjoy really getting to know one town and region, as well as the people there.

Several years ago, when we began thinking about spending our autumns in France, it was all about the adventures we were going to have along the way. Now it had morphed into being much more about the friends we have made in our village. Chip often says that everyone tells me their life stories after only a brief encounter (I sometimes hear all the woes of the person at the grocery store cash register before I'm done making my purchases). Maybe for this reason or some other, we feel really connected to these people and families. Acquaintances that began in that first fall continued to grow and blossom into lasting friendships. Some friends have remained in the village; sadly other friends have moved on to other towns. Babies have been born to several of our friends, and another generation begins. We now know what we had suspected all along: in spite of different languages, cultures and beliefs, people are people, with common interests that connect us. People everywhere share love of family, caring for each other, enjoying a good meal with friends, and getting outside to see what Mother Nature has to offer. In all our travels, these are values that we have observed people share all over the world.

We have now been back to France for many extended stays in our adopted village. Now, when we depart, instead of saying to our friends "*Au revoir*" (Good-bye), we just say "*À la prochaine*" - Until next time.

Appendix 1- France Beyond Burgundy

We have primarily focused our attention in this book on the Burgundy area of France. There are, however, some other fantastically beautiful regions in which we have traveled and absolutely loved. We would be remiss not to mention them here for your consideration. There are many travel books about France and its various regions. For starters, we would recommend getting the latest version of the Rick Steves' France book.

Alsace

This area in northeastern France contains a mix of French and German cultures. In fact, many of the folks who live here speak both languages fluently. This is due to the fact that this area along the Rhine River has gone back and forth from French to German rule over the centuries. A hilly terrain shows many vineyards, castle ruins and really nice hiking trails. Anchored on the south by Colmar and the north by Strasbourg, the landscape is dotted with many small picturesque villages with half-timbered houses and restaurants with a Germanic bent. Strasbourg, the big city of the region, has a magnificent cathedral. We love the towns of Eguisheim and the slightly larger Ribeauvillé. Our favorite wine of this area is the richly flavored Alsatian Gewürztraminer. Yum!

Bordeaux

The town of Bordeaux is like a mini Paris, as it has some of the same architectural Hausmann-style buildings in its downtown area. A long-time sea port town, the river front has now been turned into a great pedestrian park. It is a very walkable town with many fine restaurants. The new wine museum, Cité du Vin, is located in a very modern building just north of the main town. Nearby, in the *région* of Bordeaux, are many fine vineyards to visit along the Garonne River.

Brittany & Normandy

These areas, just northwest of Paris, have long had influences from the British. For us, it was a great lesson in history to visit the World War II D-Day beaches and cemeteries in Normandy. A very moving experience. Another iconic site in Brittany is Mont St-Michelle with its beautiful profile. Nearer to Paris is Giverny, where Monet painted his famous water lilies. Along the coast is the picturesque town of Honfleur. The town of Bayeux shows off its famous tapestry. Rouen and its connection to Joan of Arc is also well worth a visit.

Côte d'Azur

The Mediterranean dominates here with famous towns along its shores. Nice is the big town in the area with its Promenade des Anglais and Chagall Museum. Monaco anchors the east end of the area. Fun for a visit to see how the other half lives on yachts and the famous casino. Villefranche-sur-Mer lies between the two and makes for a great home base. Near Villefranche-sur-Mer is Cap Ferrat with the beautiful Rothschild Villa to tour. Hill towns above the coast are fun to drive to and hike within. A visit to a perfume factory is a must.

Dordogne and Lot River Valley

Located in southwestern France, this area is famous for its dark and tasty Malbec wine. Towns we like are Cahors, Rocamadour and Sarlat. There are a couple of caves in the area with prehistoric paintings-Lascaux and Pech Merle. For a beautiful drive, head east along the meandering Lot River valley. One of our favorite villages along the route is Saint-Cirq-Lapopie which is perched high above the river.

French Alps

This area in eastern France features high mountains between Grenoble and Chamonix, as well as the beautiful lake town of Annecy. In and around Annecy are wonderful restaurants, boat tours on the lake, and great biking routes. A visit to Mont Blanc is a memorable trip. On the way down, take the gondola part-way and try a hike back into Chamonix. Skiing, of course, dominates the winter in this area. North of Chamonix is the lovely Lake Geneva.

Languedoc

In southern France near Spain is the Languedoc region. On the coast of the Mediterranean are some lovely towns- a couple are Béziers and Collioure- with great beaches. Inland, Carcassonne is a great place to visit with its dominating castle. Good vineyards nearby as well. Nearby, Albi has one of France's most unique and beautiful cathedrals. In the countryside are many small villages. Many of these are close to castle ruins of the Cathars that make for good hiking.

Loire Valley

What to do? Pick a town as a home base, and visit this area's famous châteaux. We enjoyed staying in Amboise, which, in addition to its proximity to many of the famous castles, had a thriving downtown. This is a terrific area for cyclists. We also spent an enjoyable day in nearby Tours. Heading back towards Paris is Chartres and its famous cathedral.

Paris

Any France travel book will tell you about the main tourist attractions to visit in the Paris. When you've checked those off your list, consider some of our other favorite things to do in this magical city. You won't regret strolling in Luxembourg Gardens, taking a walking tour in the Catacombs, touring the Palais Garnier (old Paris Opera House), finding a Jazz Manouche concert to attend, visiting the Rue Cler market and area, relaxing on an evening Seine river cruise, seeing the Impressionistic art at Musée d'Orsay, going to a concert at Sainte-Chapelle, touring Les Invalides, visiting the Père Lachaise Cemetery, or visiting the Musée National Rodin and the Musée de l'Orangerie. Of course, you can't beat just walking the city, buying a fresh croissant or pastry, or eating lunch or dinner at a sidewalk café. Find the time to sip a glass of wine at a café while watching the world go by.

Close to Paris is the town of Versailles with its famous castle and grounds. Allow the better part of a day to take some of the various tours and walk the grounds.

Also near to Paris is the town of Fontainebleau. We have often driven to this town from greater France, parked our car at the station, and taken the train into Paris. This is our way of avoiding driving in Paris proper. Also in this town is the Château de Fontainebleau. It was used, not only by the French royal families, but also by Napoleon Bonaparte, and, in a way, Pope Pius VII also lived there. The Pope was held there against his will for two years when there was a little disagreement about who was in charge of the Church in France. This chateau is smaller and less ornate than Versailles, but it is still huge, wonderfully over-decorated, and well worth a visit.

Provence

This region of lavender, olives and the famous *Mistral* wind is in southeastern France. It has been a favorite of artists over the centuries. Open expanses rule the day. Mont Ventoux, the famous climb used numerous times in the Tour de France, can dominate the sky and the drive or bike ride (not us!) up is spectacular. Among the area's many highlights are the Roman arena in Arles, the archaeological ruins in Vaison-la-Romaine, and the Pont du Gard aqueduct. Our favorite towns include Aix-en-Provence, Avignon and Sault- one of the hill towns of the Luberon.

Appendix 2- Joni's Gougères Recipe

Gougères are a delicious appetizer that we've had in French homes- they are basically a cheesy puff pastry, and are not difficult to make. I've tried several recipes for these, and for me, this recipe seems the most authentic to what we had in Burgundy. However, many recipes call for milk instead of water, and some call for more eggs. This one, a mixture of a few I tried, works for me. Have fun!

<u>Ingredients</u>

1 cup water

8 tablespoons of unsalted butter, cut into narrow slices (so that it will melt quickly in the water)

½ teaspoon salt

1 cup flour

4 eggs

1 ½ cups gruyere cheese

3 tablespoons Parmesan grated cheese

1/8 teaspoon nutmeg

¼ teaspoon black pepper

Optional: 1-2 additional tablespoons Parmesan grated cheese

Optional: 1-2 tablespoons chopped fresh herbs (possibly chives, parsley, and/or thyme)

Instructions

- Preheat oven to 375 degrees F (350 with convection).

- Line two baking sheets with parchment paper.

- Grate gruyere cheese in a food processor or by hand.

- In a saucepan, bring water, butter and salt to a rolling boil (and until all butter is melted).

- Add flour; mix with a wooden spoon for 30 seconds or so, until a sticky dough ball forms, and the dough begins to pull away from the sides of the pan.

- Reduce heat to low-medium and cook, stirring vigorously, for another 90 seconds.

- Remove from heat and set aside for five minutes.

- Beat in eggs, one at a time, off heat. Don't panic if the dough separates when each egg is added. Just keep beating with your wooden spoon, and it will turn out alright in the end. Dough should become shiny after all the eggs are in.

- Beat in, by hand, the cheeses, nutmeg and black pepper. Add chopped fresh herbs if you are using them. You may want to put pan back on a very low heat if it becomes too stiff to stir.

- Place heaping teaspoons of dough onto baking sheets, about two inches apart. Optional: sprinkle dough balls with more parmesan cheese.

• Bake for 25-30 minutes, rotating pans halfway through. The gougères are done when they are golden and puffed.

• Since they are best warm from the oven, serve immediately and amaze your guests!

About the Authors

Minnesota residents **Joni Sutton and Chip Williams** are both retired band directors and music educators. Throughout their careers, they were recognized by peer groups for their superior bands and contributions to their field. Since retiring, they have remained active as guest clinicians, and are the Tour Directors for the Minnesota Ambassadors of Music. Joni and Chip both have a passion for international travel. They have written articles for various music education publications and travel blogs.

CPSIA information can be obtained
at www.ICGtesting.com
Printed in the USA
LVHW081334151121
703381LV00013B/321